Out of Sight

First published in this form in 1999
by ScreenPress Books
28 Castle Street Eye Suffolk IP23 7AW

This edition is produced in association with
Sight and Sound Magazine. Sensibly priced to enable as much
accesibility as possible to new and dynamic screenwriting.

Photoset by Parker Typesetting Service ~~Leic~~
Printed in Scotland by
Caledonian International Book Manufacturing Ltd.

A CIP record for this book is available from
the British Library.

ISBN 1 901680 41X

For more information on forthcoming film books from
ScreenPress Books, please contact the publishers at the above address or:

fax on: 01502 725422
e-mail: *screenpressbooks@hotmail.com*
website: www.screenpress.co.uk

Out of Sight

Scott Frank

**based on the novel by
Elmore Leonard**

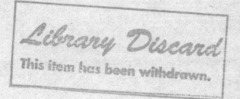

SP
SCREENPRESS BOOKS

BLACK

We hear traffic, some street noises, then . . .

FADE IN:

EXT. MIAMI STREET. DAY

The financial district. Lots of people in suits. A shaky, spasmodic zoom-in finds . . .

Jack Foley – forty, big, focused expression – as he rips a tie from around his neck and throws it down in the gutter. He starts across the street, now peeling off his suitcoat and dropping that, too, right there on the asphalt as we then . . .

Pan over to a bank across the street as Foley goes inside.

CUT TO:

A printed brochure that reads:
LOOKING FOR MONEY?
YOU'VE COME TO THE RIGHT PLACE.

We then pull back to reveal . . .

INT. BANK. DAY

Foley stands at a counter holding the above Credit Application while he studies the bank layout.

He watches a man in a suit, carrying an attaché case, enter the bank and move through the gate into the fenced-off business area at the front. An executive rises from his desk, shakes hands with the man and they both sit down.

Foley tosses the brochure in the trash, then crosses to a teller window where a nameplate on the counter tells us the young woman with the pile of dark hair smiling at him is Loretta.

3

TELLER/LORETTA

How can I help you, sir?

FOLEY

Loretta, you see that guy talking to your manager, has his case open?

Foley takes out a Zippo lighter and casually, yet expertly, begins to fiddle with it as the teller looks across the bank.

LORETTA

That's Mr Guindon, one of our assistant managers. Our manager is Mr Schoen, but he's not in today.

FOLEY

But you see the guy with the attaché case?

LORETTA
(*looks again*)

Yes.

FOLEY

That's my partner. He has a gun in there. And if you don't do exactly what I tell you, or you give me any kind of a problem, I'll look over at my partner and he'll shoot your Mr Guindon between the eyes.

Loretta goes stiff, swallows, stares back at Foley.

Now take one of those big envelopes and put as many hundreds, fifties and twenties as you can pack into it. Nothing with bank straps or rubber bands. I don't want any dye packs. I don't want any bait money. Start with the second drawer and then the one over there, under the computer. Come on, Loretta, the key's right there next to you. No bills off the bottom of the drawer.
(*as she works*)
First time being robbed?

> *(she nods)*
> You're doing great. Just smile, Loretta, so you won't look
> like you're being held up.
> > *(she smiles awkwardly)*
> That's the way, you're doing fine.

*We hear a bit of thunder and Foley cuts a fast look out the front
door. When he turns back, he sees that Loretta's having some
trouble fitting all the bills into the envelope.*

FOLEY

Here, give me the twenties. I'll put 'em in my pocket. OK, I
haven't had to give my partner a sign; that's good. Now, he's
gonna wait thirty seconds till after I'm out the door, make
sure you haven't set off the alarm. If you have, he's gonna
shoot Mr Guindon between the eyes. OK? I think that'll do
it. Thank you, Loretta, and have a nice day.

LORETTA

You, too.

*Foley heads for the door. He pauses by Mr Guindon's desk,
looks back at Loretta. Foley smiles at her, then turns to the man
sitting with Mr Guindon, indicates Loretta . . .*

FOLEY

She's cute, isn't she?

The man looks across the bank at Loretta.

MAN

Uh, yeah, I guess so.

Foley winks at Loretta and walks out.

> *(to Mr Guindon)*
> Who was that?

EXT. BANK. DAY

*As Foley comes out, he calmly walks to a Honda Civic and gets
in.*

INT. CAR. DAY

Foley tries to start the car. No go. He tries again.

                    FOLEY
Come on . . .

But the car won't start. Foley bangs on the wheel.

Fuck!

*Foley then stiffens as a cop sticks his gun through the open
window into Foley's ear.*

                    COP
I think you flooded it.

*Foley looks to the passenger window, where another cop,
smiling, now has his gun pointing at him.*

                  SECOND COP
Get out've the car, sir.

                    FOLEY
Wanna hear a funny story?

                  SECOND COP
Shut up and get out of the car.

And as Foley obliges, we then . . .

FADE TO WHITE

*We hear a man grunt. Then see Foley in slow motion as he jumps
through frame; now we see a basketball come up in his hand as
we realize he's on his way to the rim when . . .*

Another guy rams into him in mid-air, knocks him down.

EXT. PRISON YARD. DAY

*A basketball game in progress. All of the men, Foley included,
are dressed in blue coveralls and white T-shirts. The game is
rough. Hair is pulled. Eyes are poked. Faces punched.*

A title reads: GLADES CORRECTIONAL INSTITUTION.

BELLE GLADE, FLORIDA.

Foley is the oldest player here. He's getting tired, starts to lose his breath. He finally walks off the court, breathing so hard he can't even talk. He simply motions to some young convict to come in and take his place.

Foley sits down on a bench, tries to catch his breath. He looks across the yard to where a group of elderly inmates sitting around a wooden picnic table are playing cards. All of them are over sixty. One of them, a one-legged guy on crutches, hops away from the table, spits out some tobacco.

Intercut the old-timers with Foley watching them.

One old guy is making a picture frame out of old Pall Mall and Lucky Strike packets. Another tends to a tomato bush in a tiny patch of garden near the wall. Another one sits nearby, painting a picture of a man and a boy fishing from a rowing boat.

Foley is about to get up off the bench when something catches his eye. He watches as two Latino men, both little guys, jog past the game, slow to a walk, then stop and begin stretching out. One of them nods to Foley. Foley nods back, waits for the Latin guys to walk off, then walks over to a guard, Pupko ('Pup'), heavy-set, dumb as dirt.

> PUP
>
> You want something, Foley?

Foley keeps his eyes fixed on the basketball game.

> FOLEY
>
> Some people are going out of here. What if I told you where and when?

> PUP
>
> How many?

> FOLEY
>
> I expect you to look out for me, Pup, let me run off work details.

PUP

OK. How many going out?

FOLEY

I hear six.

PUP

When?

FOLEY

Looks like tonight.

PUP

You know who they are?

FOLEY

I do, but I won't tell you just yet. Meet me in the chapel at eight-thirty, right before lock-down.

INT. MESS HALL. DAY

As Foley takes his lunch tray up the centre aisle, he scans the sea of white T-shirts until he sees the two little Latins sitting at a table full of other little Latins. Chino – fifties, in shape – shovels macaroni in his mouth.

Chino's 'wife', Lulu, nineteen, looks up from his own neat tray of macaroni and jello and watches Foley walk past and sit down with a bunch of bikers.

Foley watches as the guy across from Chino scrapes some macaroni off his plate and on to Chino's and Chino wolfs that down, too.

EXT. MESS. DAY

Chino steps outside and lights a cigarette. He puts an arm around Lulu, starts to walk off . . .

FOLEY
(off-screen)

Today's the day, huh?

8

Chino looks over, watches Foley approach, lets his arm slip down so he can hook his thumb into Lulu's belt – the next thing to having him on a leash.

You excited?

CHINO

I told you, man, Super Bowl Sunday.

FOLEY

Yeah, but I see you moved it up.

CHINO
(*beat*)

Why you think is today?

FOLEY

You were out running this morning, sticking to your routine, anybody happened to notice. But you only did a couple of miles instead of your usual five. Saving yourself for the main event. Then I see you inside eating ten pounds of macaroni. Carbohydrates for endurance.

Chino and Lulu exchange looks.

CHINO

You want, I tole you you can come. You all right, Foley. I like you.

FOLEY

You told me I can come 'cause I caught you digging the fuckin' tunnel, saw you and Lulu coming out of the bushes, thought maybe you two were making out.

Foley smiles at Lulu, who glares back at him.

So what, you finish ahead of schedule?

Chino looks towards the fence along the front of the yard.

CHINO

You see what they doing, those posts out there? Putting up another fence, five metres on the other side of the one that's there. We wait until Super Bowl Sunday, they could have the second fence built and we have to dig another nine, ten days. So we going soon as it's dark. You want – I mean it – you can still come.

FOLEY

I appreciate the offer. And it's tempting.

Foley looks off towards the visitors' parking area, the fence not twenty yards away.

But, man, it's a long run to civilization. A hundred miles to Miami? I'm too old to start acting crazy, try a stunt like that. You make it out, send me a postcard.

CUT TO:

A notepad where we see someone has written 'IT'S MAGIC!' then crossed out the 'IT'S' and replaced it with the word 'LIKE'. We hear the phone ring and . . .

INT. ADELE'S APARTMENT. DAY

Miami Beach Moderne. Adele – mid-thirties, pretty, Foley's ex – sits at her kitchen table writing on a pad. She grabs the phone.

ADELE

Hello?
(*then sighs*)
Yeah, I accept.

INT. PRISON HALLWAY. DAY

Foley on the phone.

FOLEY'S VOICE

Hey, Adele, how you doing?

Intercutting Foley and Adele:

ADELE

Hey, Bank Robber, want some advice? Next time, leave the engine running.

FOLEY

That's funny, Adele. How many more times you gonna gimme that one?

ADELE

Till it's not funny any more. What do you want, Jack?

FOLEY

You know that Super Bowl party? They changed the date. It's on *tonight*, eight-thirty.

ADELE

Didn't you tell me one-time calls aren't monitored?

FOLEY

I said not as a rule.

ADELE

So why don't you come right out and tell me what you're talking about?

FOLEY

Listen to Miss Smarty Mouth. Out there in the free world.

ADELE

What's free about it? I'm looking for work.

FOLEY

What happened to Mandrake the Magician?

ADELE

Emil the Amazing. The bastard fired me and hired another girl, a redhead. I'm working on a new business card, pass out to the cafés. How's this sound –

FOLEY
(*cuts her off*)

Listen, Adele, the reason I called, that party is today instead of Sunday. About eight-thirty, like only a few hours from now. So you'll have to get hold of Buddy, whatever he might be doing.

ADELE

And the one driving the other car?

FOLEY

What're you talking about?

ADELE

Well, seeing as you have so much luck with cars, Buddy
thought it might be better to bring two. He got this guy he
says you know from Lompoc, Glenn something.

FOLEY

Glenn Michaels.

ADELE

Yeah, that's him. Buddy says Glenn thinks you guys are real
cool.

FOLEY

He did, huh. Well, tell Buddy I see Glenn wearing his
sunglasses, I'll step on 'em. I might not even take 'em off
first.

INT. RESTAURANT. DAY

*Marshall Sisco – fifty – slides a small wrapped box across a
table . . .*

MARSHALL

Happy birthday.

*. . . to where Karen Sisco – twenty-eight, black suit, long hair, a
knockout – sits. She picks up the box and shakes it.*

KAREN

You fit another Chanel suit in here?

MARSHALL

Something better. Open it.

*Karen starts to carefully unwrap the present. Marshall watches,
takes a sip of his drink, looks around the bar, sees how
everyone's looking at the two of them . . .*

KAREN
(opens the box)

Oh my God . . .

She pulls a gleaming automatic pistol from the box . . .

It's beautiful.

MARSHALL

It's a –

KAREN

– Sig-Sauer .38. I love it.

She leans across the table and kisses him.

Thanks, Dad.

MARSHALL

Happy birthday, kid.
(pause)
You want another Coke?

KAREN
(checks her watch)
Can't. I gotta drive out to Glades, then I'm meeting Ray
Nicolet at ten.

MARSHALL

Which one is that? The ATF guy?

KAREN

He was. Ray's with the FBI now, he switched over.

MARSHALL

He's still married though, huh?

KAREN

Technically. They're separated.

MARSHALL

Oh, he's moved out?

KAREN

He's about to.

MARSHALL

Then they're not separated, are they?

KAREN

Can we change the subject?

MARSHALL

What're you doing at Glades?

KAREN

Serving process, a Summons and Complaint. Some con doing mandatory life doesn't like macaroni and cheese. He files suit, says he has no choice in what they serve and it violates his civil rights.

MARSHALL

You know you can always step in, work with me full-time as one of my investigators.

KAREN

No thanks.

MARSHALL

You used to like it.

KAREN

Dad . . .

MARSHALL

You'd meet doctors, lawyers – nothing wrong with them necessarily if they're divorced. Why settle for some cowboy cop who drinks too much and cheats on his wife? That's the way those hotshots are, all of 'em.

KAREN

I really gotta go.

MARSHALL

We don't get to talk much any more.

KAREN

How 'bout I come next Sunday and watch the Super Bowl with you?

MARSHALL

I'd like that.

She gets up, kisses him again.

KAREN

Thanks for the gun, Dad.

INT. FOLEY'S CELL. BELLE GLADE. DAY

*Foley comes in, lies down on the bunk. He looks about the cell.
All he's got to show for himself. It's now quiet on the cellblock.
He closes his eyes.*

CUT TO:

A PRISON AUDITORIUM

*A few hundred cons scream encouragement/insults as Maurice
'Snoopy' Miller, a lanky, scary, mean-looking black man in
boxing trunks, hits a white guy with a ferocious hook.*

A title reads: LOMPOC FEDERAL PENITENTIARY,
LOMPOC, CALIFORNIA. *And then:* TWO YEARS AGO.

*At the back of the auditorium Foley leans in a doorway watching
with Buddy Bragg – black, Foley's age, shaved head.*

*The bell sounds and the white guy staggers to his corner, as does
Maurice. Glenn Michaels – surfer look, dark shades – counts cash
in Maurice's corner, whispers something into the fighter's ear.*

BUDDY

Ref don't call it pretty soon, Snoopy's gonna send this guy
out in a body bag.

*Foley watches a man – fifties, out of place, not as hard-looking as
those around him. The guy looks nervous, can feel the other
cons' eyes on him as he tries to find a seat.*

*The bell sounds and the white boxer staggers to his feet. Maurice
steps in and resumes the bloody pummelling. Foley turns and
watches the fight now.*

FOLEY

Anyone ever tell you why they call him Snoopy?

Buddy shakes his head. Maurice dances around the other guy now. Teases him.

He was Maurice 'Mad Dog' Miller back when he was pro. Now you pet him, he goes down.

The white guy throws a tired, loping roundhouse that barely glances off Maurice's jaw. Sure enough, Maurice makes a big show out of snapping his head back, staggering, before he finally goes down.

BUDDY

I don't believe it.

Foley watches the new inmate as fights erupt all around him and, anxious now, he tries to get out of there.

EXT. PRISON YARD. DAY

Foley and Buddy sit atop a cement picnic table watching as, nearby, the 'winning' boxer – still wearing last night's pummelling on his face – gloats to a group of cons. He throws a fake punch at one of them as he demonstrates his winning technique.

BUDDY

Guy's braggin' he won a thrown fight. Fuckin' pathetic.

Foley looks at the other side of the yard, where Maurice now stands at the far side, coldly watching the guy, one hand thrust into his pocket. Foley watches as Maurice stops the new inmate – the older guy who looked out of place at the fight – as he comes out into the yard.

FOLEY

It's Richard Ripley.

BUDDY
(looking now)

The Wall Street guy? Oh, yeah. I didn't recognize him without his rug.

Foley watches as Maurice talks to the new inmate, the guy nodding, acquiescent, respectful.

> FOLEY

Dick the Ripper they called him, on account of all the people he ripped off.

Foley watches as Ripley now makes a note in a black book.

> BUDDY

What's he doin' here?

> GLENN
> (*off-screen*)

Three years.

They look to where Glenn Michaels, the blond guy in dark shades we saw in Maurice's corner, works out on the bench press a few feet away. He's shirtless, tanned, in shape.

He got three years and fined fifty million dollars and wrote 'em a fucking cheque. Like that, fifty mil, signed his name.
> (*struggles with the bar*)

Whoa – little help here!

> FOLEY

Who you talkin' to, Studs? Me, or Buddy. I can't tell, you got those shades on.

> GLENN

You guys – come on – this is too heavy!

> FOLEY

I guess the bright glare out here made it hard to see the numbers on the weights.

> GLENN

I'll take the shades off. Just get this fuckin' thing off me.

Foley helps him get the bar up. Glenn sits up.

> BUDDY

How do you know he wrote a cheque?

GLENN

He told me. He works the laundry with me. The guy loves to talk.

FOLEY

Yeah, to the US Attorney. I hear he rolled over on all the snitches he was doing business with and got 'em all brought up.

He watches Snoopy talking to Ripley, one eye always on the swaggering boxer across the yard, one hand in his pocket.

GLENN

Hey, anybody that can write a cheque for fifty mil, he says *any*thing, I'm all fucking ears. Like the other day, he tells me how he's got all this money in foreign banks, plus around five mil in uncut diamonds at his house. He said, quote, 'Where I can put my hands on it anytime.'

BUDDY

Cool. Where's the guy live?

Foley watches a few more of Maurice's friends surround Ripley. Again, Ripley takes out his black book, starts nodding, making notations.

GLENN

Detroit. Snoopy Miller told me uncut diamonds are as easy to move as cash.

FOLEY

Ever seen an uncut diamond, Studs? They look like plain old rocks.

GLENN

So. What's your point?

FOLEY

My point is, that's probably what you're gonna end up with.

GLENN

You think he's lying?

FOLEY
Use your head. The guys got five million lying around his house, you really think he's gonna tell some motormouth he just met in prison about it?

A bell sounds. Everyone starts walking for the gate.

Foley watches as the boxer and his crew head for the gate, Maurice still standing there with his hand in his pocket.

Slow motion as the boxer gets to the gate, sees Maurice, who moves to him now, smiling like he's so glad to see him . . . his left hand clapping the guy on the back, saying something like 'congratulations' as now his right hand comes out of his pocket and we see the long metal shiv –

BUDDY
(*watching Snoopy*)
Here it comes.

Maurice wraps his left arm around the boxer's shoulder and hugs him tight for a moment, then quickly moves away. The boxer stands there like a statue, doesn't move until he's at last jostled from behind and his legs fold and he drops to the cement.

I guess the Snoop doesn't like to lose, even if it's on purpose.

We hear a whistle blow as a guard spots the body. And now everyone moves like hell for the gate . . . except for . . .

Richard Ripley, who stands there frozen, staring down at the body.

Foley glances back at the approaching guards, casually takes Ripley by the arm as he passes, leads him away from there, talks to him as they walk into the block . . .

FOLEY
You don't wanna be standing there, the hacks start asking questions you don't wanna answer.

RIPLEY
Oh, uh, right, thanks . . .

Foley then moves away. He sees Maurice looking back at him, giving him a hard stare just before he melts into the crowd.

DISSOLVE TO:

INT. FOLEY'S CELL. BELLE GLADE. DAY (NOW)

He lies there another moment when . . .

. . . a pair of legs swings down over the side from the top bunk. Foley's cellmate jumps down, walks the three feet or so to the toilet, casually pulls down his pants and starts to go to the bathroom. Foley shakes his head and turns away.

EXT. STRIP MALL. DAY

Buddy walks up to a Cadillac Sedan DeVille Concours pulling a slim-jim from the back of his pants, about to jimmy the door, when he sees . . .

. . . a woman – middle-aged, wearing pearls and high heels – come out of the Winn Dixie pushing a grocery cart full of groceries.

Buddy sticks the jimmy back in his pants, waits until the woman is opening her trunk before coming forward.

> BUDDY
> Here, lemme help you with those, ma'am.

She doesn't seem too sure about it, but lets him load the groceries in the trunk and take the key out of the lock.

> WOMAN
> I didn't ask for your help, so don't expect a tip.

Buddy smiles, waves her off.

> BUDDY
> That's OK, ma'am. I'll just take your car.

She stands there stupidly as he gets in and drives off.

INT. CHAPEL. DUSK

In the midst of a remodel. As door opens and Pup comes in, Foley puts a finger to his lips.

> FOLEY
> They're right underneath you, Pup. They dug a tunnel.

Foley watches Pup creep up the aisle towards the front of the chapel, eyes on the floor, listening . . .

> PUP
> I don't hear 'em. Where's the tunnel come out?

Pup turns his back, walks up the aisle and across the front of the pews to a window.

> FOLEY
> Second fence post from the tower out there. Go on, take a look.

As Pup stares out the window . . .

> PUP
> I don't see nothing there.

Foley reaches down into a pew where's stashed a four-foot crucifix. He picks it up, starts up the aisle . . .

> FOLEY
> You will directly. Keep watching.

INT. KAREN SISCO'S CAR. DUSK

The high beams from her car show the prison parking area, then the fence strung with razor wire. Karen parks near the fence, lights a cigarette and dials her car phone.

> KAREN
> Hi. Karen Sisco again for Ray Nicolet.
> *(beat)*
> He's not? Could you tell him that . . . never mind. I'll call back.

Headlights hit Karen's rear-view mirror, a car pulling in behind her. The lights go off, then come on again. She adjusts the mirror to deflect the glare.

INT. THE CAR BEHIND HER. DUSK

Buddy sits watching the cons come in from the athletic field. He sees the mirror flash in the car in front of him as Karen checks her face out in the rear-view.

INT. CHAPEL. DUSK

As Foley moves up behind Pup, he lets his jacket fall to the floor, holds the crucifix down against his leg.

> PUP
> There some car headlights out there . . .
> > (*then*)
> Jesus Christ . . .

Now he pulls his radio from his belt, says into it . . .

> Man outside the fence! By tower six!
> > (*responds to radio*)
> This is Officer Pupko . . .
> > (*then*)
> I'm looking at him, for Christ's sake!

OK – now Foley raises the metal cross, steps in and lays it smack against the side of Pup's head. Drops him clean with one swing, bouncing him off the window frame and down without a sound coming from him.

INT. KAREN SISCO'S CAR. DUSK

As Karen grabs the court papers off the seat, she opens her car door, glances at the fence and pauses as she sees a figure there, crouching down.

Karen turns on her headlights. No, not crouched. The guy is coming out of the ground. On this side of the fence.

Head and shoulders appear and another guy comes out of the ground. Right in front of her.

Karen leans on the horn, holds it down and sees the two guys by the fence – Chino and Lulu – look into her headlights, poised there for a moment before taking off into the dark. Karen gets out of the car.

INT. BUDDY'S CAR. DUSK

As Buddy watches a spotlight from the tower come on and follow the two cons, we then hear the sound of rifle reports before the men disappear into the dark.

Then Buddy sees Karen in his headlights, whistles softly as he gets a good look at her long legs as she raises the lid to her trunk . . .

> BUDDY
> What's she doing?

He watches her duck her head in the trunk and come out with a holstered pistol.

> Uh-oh.

But then she throws the pistol in the trunk, ducks in there again and comes out this time racking a shotgun.

> Uh-oh.

And now Buddy watches her hurry to the front of her car and raise the shotgun as we hear a whistle blow in the compound. Buddy gets out of the car.

EXT. PARKING AREA. DUSK

Karen puts the shotgun on two more cons, both filthy dirty, standing by the hole they just crawled out of.

> KAREN
> Get your hands in the air!

Buddy watches the two cons, both Latins, make up their minds, start edging away – shit, they've come this far.

They look out at the spotlight sweeping around in the dark, then look the other way, along the fence towards the main gate, to see armed hacks coming out on the run, and that decides it for the cons. They take off running.

Now Buddy watches as Karen puts her pump gun on them, but doesn't fire.

The hacks running from the gate with rifles beat her to it, open all at once and keep firing until the two convicts are cut down as they run.

The hacks glance at Karen, but don't bother with her, more interested in the hole the convicts had come out of. Now they're standing by it peering in, edging closer with their weapons ready; then they step back at once, bump into each other as . . .

A head appears wearing a guard's baseball cap, the guy now saying something to the guards, his face smeared with muck, excited, pointing towards the orange grove.

They run off, pausing briefly to kick the convicts they shot to see if they're alive, then keep going.

The man in the hole, Foley, climbs out. He takes his time, puts on a show, standing with his hands on his hips like an honest-to-God hack, that serious cap down on his eyes.

Buddy waves to Foley to come on and Karen turns and puts the shotgun on Buddy. Buddy raises the palm of his hand.

BUDDY

It's OK, honey, we're good guys.

KAREN

What're you doing here?

Not so much asking, but putting it to him the way cops do when they're already pretty sure what you're doing. She glances around to include Foley, now coming at her like some creature out of the swamp, giving Buddy time to take her around the neck.

She fights him, jabs him in the gut with the butt end of the shotgun before Foley wrenches it from her grip.

They drag her to the rear end of her car, the trunk lid still up, and crouch there as some hacks come running along the fence, past the dark gun tower and cross the road towards the orange grove. A moment later, they hear bursts of gunfire, then silence.

FOLEY

I bet that's all the hacks they send out. Otherwise nobody's left to mind the store.

BUDDY

Why don't we talk about it later?

He turns to see Foley and Karen staring at each other in the headlights from Buddy's car; Karen not at all afraid.

FOLEY

Why, you're just a girl. What do you do for a living you pack a shotgun?

KAREN

I'm a federal marshal and you're under arrest, both of you guys.

Foley keeps staring at her like he's giving the situation serious thought, but what he says is . . .

FOLEY

I bet I smell, don't I?

(pause)

Listen, you hop in the trunk and we'll get out of here.

Karen looks at him, then gets up, climbs into the trunk. She's reaching around, trying to find her pistol, when . . .

Foley gives her a shove and gets in with her, wedging her against the wall of the trunk, pressing against her back like they're cuddled up in bed.

He holds her to him, giving her no room to turn and stick the gun in his face. Buddy reaches for the trunk lid and then everything goes . . .

BLACK

Total darkness, not a crack or a pinpoint of light showing. Then we hear the engine come to life, the car moving along.

> FOLEY
> (*voice-over*)
>
> You comfy?

> KAREN
> (*voice-over*)
> If I could have a little more room.

> FOLEY
> (*voice-over*)
> There isn't any. All this shit you got in here. What is all this stuff anyway? Handcuffs, chains . . . what's this can?

> KAREN
> (*voice-over*)
> For your breath. You could use it. Squirt some in your mouth.

> FOLEY
> (*voice-over*)
> You devil, it's mace, huh? What've you got here, a billy? Use it on poor unfortunate offenders.

A beam of light appears as he finds a flashlight and turns it on. He plays the beam along Karen's leg, calms down some as he looks at all of her now and finally says . . .

> Where's your gun, your pistol?

> KAREN
>
> In my bag, in the car.

They go over some bumps. We hear men's voices from somewhere far off, outside.

> You know you don't have a chance of making it. Guards are out here already, they'll stop the car.

He runs his hand down her thigh, looking for her gun, but also, just, well, looking.

26

FOLEY

They're off in the cane by now chasing Cubans. I timed it to slip between the cracks, you might say.

EXT. CAR. NIGHT

Buddy floors it away from the prison, checks the rear-view mirror.

INT. TRUNK. NIGHT

Foley tries to wipe some of the mud off his face.

FOLEY

Boy, it stunk in there.

KAREN

I believe it. You've ruined a nine-hundred-dollar suit my dad gave me.

FOLEY

Yeah, went real nice with that twelve-gauge, too.
(*pause*)
Tell me, why in the world would someone like you ever become a federal marshal?

KAREN

The idea of going after guys like you appealed to me.

FOLEY

Guys like me, huh. Well, listen, even though I've been celibate lately, I'm not gonna force myself on you. I've never done that in my life.

KAREN

You wouldn't have time anyway. We come to a roadblock, they'll run the car, find out in five seconds who it belongs to.

FOLEY

If they get set up in time, which I doubt. And even if they do they'll be looking for a buncha little Latin fellas, not a big black guy driving a Ford.

> KAREN

Must be quite a pal, risk his own ass like this.

More bumps. Then picking up speed as the road smooths out.

> FOLEY

Who, Buddy? Yeah. He's a good guy. Back when we jailed together, he'd call his sister every week without fail. She's a born-again Christian, does book-keeping for a televangelist. Buddy calls her up, confesses his sins, tells her about whatever bank he happened to rob.

> KAREN

Buddy. That's his given name?

> FOLEY
> *(whoops, beat)*

One I gave him, yeah.
> *(mouths)*

Fuck . . .

INT. CAR. NIGHT

Buddy rifles through Karen's bag while he drives. He looks up from her badge and ID case at the road.

INT. TRUNK. NIGHT

> KAREN

So, what's *your* name? It'll be in the paper tomorrow anyway.

> FOLEY

Jack Foley. You've probably heard of me.

> KAREN

Why, are you famous?

> FOLEY

Time I was convicted in California? FBI told me I'd robbed more banks than anyone in the computer.

KAREN

How many was that?

FOLEY

Tell you the truth, I don't know. I started when I was eighteen, driving for my Uncle Cully and his partner, Gus. They go into a bank this one time in Slidell, Gus jumps the counter to get to the tellers and breaks his leg. All three of us ended up in Angola.

KAREN

That's funny.

FOLEY

I thought so, too.

KAREN

It was me, I woulda left ol' Gus on the floor.

FOLEY

I believe you would have. Another fall, I did seven years at Lompoc. And I don't mean the place next door where some of Nixon's people went.

KAREN

I know the difference. You were in Lompoc USP, the federal penitentiary. I've delivered people there. So basically you've spent half your life in prison.

FOLEY
(beat)

Basically. Yeah. If I go back now, I do a full thirty years, no time off. Can you imagine looking at that?

KAREN

I don't have to. I don't rob banks.

He looks at her, then looks away.

EXT. CAR. NIGHT

The car turns into a main highway.

INT. TRUNK. NIGHT

Foley plays the light down the length of her.

> FOLEY
>
> You don't seem all that scared.

> KAREN
>
> Of course I am.

> FOLEY
>
> You don't act like it.

> KAREN
>
> What do you want me to do? Scream? I don't think it would
> help much.
> > *(pause)*
> I'm just gonna sit back, take it easy, and wait for you to
> screw up.

> FOLEY
>
> Jesus, you sound like my ex-wife.

> KAREN
>
> You were married? All those falls, I'm surprised you had
> time.

> FOLEY
>
> It was just a year, give or take a few days. I mean, it's not
> like we didn't get along or anything. We had fun, we just
> didn't have that . . . that thing, you know? That spark, you
> know what I mean? You gotta have that.

> KAREN
> > *(thinking)*
> Uh-huh.

> FOLEY
>
> We still talk, though.

> KAREN
>
> Sure.

EXT. CAR. NIGHT

Buddy passes a sign that says 'MIAMI, 74 MILES'.

INT. TRUNK. NIGHT

Karen tries to get a look at Foley.

> KAREN
> You know, this isn't gonna end well, these thing never do.

> FOLEY
> Yeah, well, if it turns out I get shot like a dog, it'll be in the street, not off a goddamn fence.

> KAREN
> You must see yourself as some kind of Clyde Barrow.

And for a few moments, all we hear is the sound of the car on the road. Then . . .

> FOLEY
> Oh, you mean of Bonnie and Clyde? Hm. You ever see pictures of him, the way he wore his hat? You could tell he had that don't-give-a-shit air about him.

> KAREN
> I don't recall his hat, but I've seen pictures of him lying dead, shot by Texas Rangers. Did you know he didn't have his shoes on?

> FOLEY
> Is that right?

> KAREN
> They put a hundred-and-eighty-seven bullet holes in Clyde, Bonnie Parker and the car they were driving. Bonnie was eating a sandwich.

> FOLEY
> You're full of interesting facts, aren't you?

> KAREN
> It was May 1934, near Gibsland, Louisiana.

EXT. HIGHWAY. NIGHT

Quiet. Empty. A moment later a car flies past.

INT. TRUNK. NIGHT

> FOLEY
>
> That part in the movie where they get shot? Warren Beatty and . . . I can't think of her name.

> KAREN
>
> Faye Dunaway.

> FOLEY
>
> Yeah, I liked her in that movie about TV . . .

> KAREN
>
> *Network*. Yeah, she was good.

> FOLEY
>
> And the guy saying he wasn't gonna take any more shit from anybody . . .

> KAREN
>
> Peter Finch.

> FOLEY
>
> Yeah, right. Anyway, that scene where Warren Beatty and Faye Dunaway get shot? I remember thinking at the time it wouldn't be a bad way to go, if you have to.

> KAREN
>
> Bleeding on a country road.

> FOLEY
>
> It wasn't pretty after, no, but if you were in that car – eating a sandwich – you wouldn't have known what hit you.

We hear faint sirens off-screen . . .

INT. CAR. NIGHT

Buddy sees flashing lights approach from the opposite direction.

He stays cool as the green-and-whites get closer . . . closer . . . then fly right on past.

INT. TRUNK. NIGHT

The sirens scream at us for a moment, then fade.

> FOLEY
>
> You're sure easy to talk to. I wonder – say we met under different circumstances and got to talking, say you were in a bar and I came up to you – I wonder what would happen.

> KAREN
>
> Nothing.

> FOLEY
>
> I mean if you didn't know who I was.

> KAREN
>
> You'd probably tell me.

> FOLEY
>
> I'm just saying I think if we met under different circumstances . . .

> KAREN
>
> You have to be kidding.

Silence. Foley tries to get back to where it was working . . .

> FOLEY
>
> Another one Faye Dunaway was in I liked, *Three Days of the Condor.*

> KAREN
>
> With Robert Redford, when he was young.

> FOLEY
>
> Yeah . . .

They lie there a moment, thinking about that, as we hear the car slowing down, coasting, then bumping along the shoulder of the road to a stop.

KAREN

I never thought it made sense, though, the way they got
together so quick.

FOLEY

Really.

KAREN

I mean, romantically.

FOLEY

Uh-huh.

(*pause*)

Well, but if –

The trunk goes dark again as the car's turned off.

BUDDY
(*off-screen*)

You still alive in there?

*And the trunk lid raises so that we see Karen and Foley lying in
the back. Foley gets out. Karen doesn't move.*

FOLEY
(*off-screen*)

Where in the hell are we?

BUDDY

That's the turnpike up there. Glenn's waiting with the other
car.

FOLEY

OK, honey, come on out of there.

*Karen pushes off, rolls from her right side to her left, brings up
her Sig-Sauer in both hands to put it on them, both standing in
the opening, in the dark, but right there.*

KAREN

Get your hands up and turn around. *Now.*

FOLEY

Shit . . .

Foley brings the lid down, he and Buddy moving in opposite directions as she begins firing from the inside . . .

Buddy and Foley hook up again in front of the car. We can see they're beneath an overpass. Foley stares at the trunk.

BUDDY

We may as well leave her. We're leaving the car and we gotta leave her some place anyway. What's the difference where?

FOLEY

She's coming with us.

Foley walks to the passenger seat, reaches in the window.

BUDDY

Jesus Christ, what were you doing in there?

FOLEY

Get the shotgun. And her purse. I'd like to know who she is.

Foley takes her wallet, looks at her driver's licence photo.

BUDDY

I already looked. Her name is Karen Sisco. Like the Cisco Kid only spelled different, S-i-s-c-o.

A sheriff's green-and-white goes screaming past and they keep to the narrow space between the car and the concrete abutment of the overpass. When the road quietens down, Foley moves to the trunk and bangs on it once with his fist.

FOLEY

Karen? Be a good girl now, you hear? Now, I'm gonna open the –

Foley jumps at the sound of a pistol shot.

You're putting holes in your car!

He looks up to see Buddy holding her shotgun, staring at him. He settles down, then . . .

We're not leaving you. I'm gonna open the trunk enough for you to throw the gun out. OK? You shoot – Buddy's got

your shotgun, says he'll shoot back if you do and I can't stop
him. So it's up to you.

*Foley puts his hand out and Buddy, still looking at him funny,
gives him the keys.*

> **VOICE**
>
> Hey!

Coming from somewhere above them.

> It's me, Glenn.

*Foley steps out into the open, Buddy close behind him. They look
up to see a figure, head and shoulders against the evening sky,
leaning on the concrete overpass rail. We can see his long blond
hair falling beside his face, now half-concealed behind dark
sunglasses.*

> **GLENN**
>
> Hey, Jack, good to see you, man. The fuck're you guys
> shooting at?

Foley looks at Buddy.

> **FOLEY**
>
> Do we need him?

> **BUDDY**
>
> The green-and-whites saw us. One of 'em starts thinking,
> what's that car doing there? Ties it to the break and turns
> around . . .

Foley thinks about it, then looks up at the overpass again.

> **FOLEY**
>
> Oh, hey, Studs? We thought you were somebody else.

> **GLENN**
>
> Studs. Man, I haven't heard that since Lompoc. What's
> going on?

> **FOLEY**
>
> Oh, nuthin'.

Foley shakes his head, then walks back to the Ford and bangs on the trunk.

You coming out?

Foley sticks the key in the lock as Buddy steps up to the trunk and racks the pump on the shotgun. Foley leans close to the metal.

You hear that?

He turns the key and raises the lid. Karen, bunched in there, extends her arm, her hand holding the Sig-Sauer by the barrel.

KAREN

You win, Jack.

'Jack.' Buddy gives him another funny look.

EXT. TOP OF OVERPASS. NIGHT

Glenn removes a note stuck in the side window of a stolen Audi that reads 'GONE TO GET GAS'.

FOLEY
(off-screen)
Have your clothes cleaned and send me the bill.

Glenn looks over as the three of them reach the top of the slope and move through the scrub. Glenn leans against the car, flashers blinking.

KAREN
I'll sent it to you at Glades.

GLENN
Jesus, what'd you crawl through, a sewer?

FOLEY
Take your sunglasses off.

GLENN
I see better with them on.

FOLEY

You don't take 'em off, I'm gonna throw 'em off the
overpass while they're still on your head.

Glenn shrugs, takes them off and sticks them in his jeans.

Wait in the car.

GLENN

You're in civilization now, man, ease up.

FOLEY

I'd like you to go wait in the car. How's that? Take her with
you and put her in back.

GLENN

In the trunk?

FOLEY

The back seat.

Foley stares at him, waiting. Glenn motions to Karen.

GLENN

Come on. I have to do what I'm told.

She walks past Foley without looking at him.

FOLEY

Wait a minute. Let me have your raincoat.
            (*looks at Buddy*)
Somebody forgot to bring me clean clothes.

BUDDY

I brought 'em, they're back at Glades in the Cadillac. You
wanted to take her car.

KAREN

You can blame me if you want. I don't mind.

*He doesn't say anything as Glenn takes off the raincoat, folds it
up, then throws it at Foley's feet.*

GLENN

Here you are, sir.

Foley watches as Glenn gets his sunglasses out, puts them back on and takes Karen by the arm.

BUDDY
What's wrong with you?

Karen looks over at Foley, then ducks her head and gets in the back seat.

FOLEY
Why you brought Glenn into this, I'll never know.

BUDDY
How 'bout the score was his idea to begin with?

FOLEY
His idea? Gimme a break. Fuckin' guy's got a vacant lot for a head. Was you and me figured the whole thing out.

Buddy watches Foley struggle with the buttons on the uniform, all of them caked with muck.

BUDDY
You're pulling at it. Here . . .

He lays the shotgun in the grass and comes up, takes the guard shirt in his two hands and rips it open, popping buttons and tearing the shirt.

FOLEY
I don't know why, but every time he opens his mouth I want to punch him out.

BUDDY
He ain't the problem, Jack.

Foley looks at him.

You wanna pull your head outta your ass and tell me why we're bringing *her* with us?

INT. CAR. NIGHT

Karen watches Glenn get into the car, sees him as the dome light comes on for a second or two before he closes the door. He half-turns, laying his arm along the top of the seats, runs his hand through his hair . . .

GLENN

. . . if he thinks he can talk to me like this. Shit, I don't even know what I need them for.

Karen leans forward to have a look. Sees Foley and Buddy against the dark foliage.

I got a big score lined up up north. They wouldn't even know about it, it wasn't for me. I could do it right now myself, except it's so fucking cold up there in January –

KAREN

Glenn?

His head turns so that we can see his designer shades.

You don't remember me, do you?

GLENN
(*beat*)
It couldn't have been out at Glades, if that's what you're thinking. I was never out there.

KAREN

No, that's not what I'm thinking.

He raises his hand, strokes his hair away from his face.

GLENN

But you're sure we've met, huh?

KAREN

Last fall, I drove you from the Palm Beach county jail to the federal courthouse, twice. You're Glenn Michaels.
(*pause*)
I never forget anyone I've cuffed and shackled.

He doesn't move or say a word, staring at her now like he's been turned to stone.

Let's think for a minute, Glenn, see if we can work this
out . . .

He turns away, all the way around to look straight ahead.

Do we have a gun in the car?

GLENN

I remember you now. Shit.

KAREN

Foley's not going to make it. And if he goes down, Glenn,
you go with him.

She touches his shoulder and he jumps.

Look, I can understand if you and Foley are close.

GLENN

We're not. I'm helping him, yeah –

KAREN

Wait. *Have* you helped him, Glenn? At this point, technically,
I doubt you could be charged with aiding a fugitive. So you
still have a choice. You can help him and risk going down
again, get cuffed and shackled, hope to God you pull a
reasonable judge, not some hard-on. Or, if you want to play it
another way . . .

She pauses. He turns and looks at her.

GLENN

Like how?

EXT. OVERPASS. NIGHT

Foley watches a car pass on the highway.

BUDDY

You want to take her to my place and get cleaned up? You
come out of the bathroom with your aftershave on and she
goes, 'Oh, I had you all wrong'?

41

FOLEY

I want to talk to her again, that's all. See what would
happen under, you know, normal circumstances.

BUDDY

You're too late, Jack.

*Foley doesn't say anything. Just takes a deep breath as we hear
the car start and they both look over.*

He wants to get out of here and I don't blame him.

*They start towards the car. Then stop and watch as it takes off,
tyres squealing as the rubber hits pavement. Their backs to us,
they stand there watching the taillights until they're out of sight
down the turnpike, neither of them saying a word.*

We hear squeaky footsteps over . . .

CUT TO:

A CORRIDOR IN LOMPOC FPC

*As Maurice Miller and his 'man' – a big black bulk named Himey
– strut purposefully up the hall.*

*They step into the prison library, where Richard Ripley sits at
one of the tables reading a big coffee-table book called* The
Warm World of Tropical Fish.

MAURICE

Dick. My man.

*Ripley looks up as Maurice and Himey come strolling into the
library and sit down on either side of a now very anxious Ripley.*

I got your fishies for you.

*He sets a small Ziploc with two tiny fish inside down on the
table.*

RIPLEY
(*reaches for them*)

Thank you . . .

MAURICE
(*pulls them back*)

Not so fast, Dick.

(*off Ripley's look*)

Starting now, there's gonna be an across the board cost a living increase.

RIPLEY

What?

MAURICE

Year ago, I come in here on credit card fraud, but after I shanked that loudmouth pussy on the yard the other day, my Dunn & Broadstreet has gone way the fuck up.

RIPLEY

I think it's Dunn & *Brad*street. But then, I could be wrong . . .

MAURICE

Whoever. The point is, prices are goin' up, too. Better get your little black book out, Richard. We got some business to talk about.

Ripley sighs, takes out his black book and opens it.

Let's start with the fish. They was two grand, but now they's three.

Ripley looks at the two tiny fish in the bag.

That Bausch & Lomb Saline shit you asked for is gonna be eighty bucks.

RIPLEY
(*writing*)

Well, I need that . . .

MAURICE

. . . and that extra pillow's gonna be an even three Cs.

VOICE

Hey.

They all look to where . . .

Jack Foley sits at the far end of the table, reading a thick manual of some kind. Himey gives him a mean stare. Foley points to a sign that says 'QUIET PLEASE'.

>   FOLEY
> Sign says 'Shut the fuck up.' Or can't you guys read?

>   MAURICE
>   (*beat*)
> There a problem, Foley?

>   FOLEY
> Yeah.

Foley shuts the big book – Chilton's Auto Repair.

>   FOLEY
> Yeah, I got a problem. This is the dumbest fucking
> shakedown in the history of dump shakedowns. Three
> hundred bucks for a pillow?

>   MAURICE
> That's right.

>   RIPLEY
> Sounds high, doesn't it?

>   FOLEY
> Must be a real soft pillow.

>   MAURICE
> Faux goose down.

>   RIPLEY
> Still . . .

>   FOLEY
> How much for your company at chow?

>   MAURICE
> Company, shit. I watch the man's back.

>   FOLEY
> I bet. How much?

44

MAURICE

Another C.

Foley shakes his head, turns to Ripley.

FOLEY

You're smart, Ripley, you'll tell this guy to fuck off.

RIPLEY

Really? Well, I uhhh . . .

FOLEY

First of all, if he kills you, he's not gonna get any more
money out of you.

Ripley looks at Maurice: good point.

MAURICE

Man doesn't have to get killed. He could accidentally fall on
something sharp, like a shiv. Or a dick.

Ripley turns back to Foley now: also a good point.

FOLEY

You stick *anything* in this guy, Snoop, they transfer his ass
outta here faster'n you can throw a fight, and you still end
up with nothing.

Ripley nods, takes this in.

MAURICE

This doesn't concern you, Foley. Why don't you go on out to
the yard, have yourself a smoke?

FOLEY

I don't smoke.

HIMEY
(*slowly rising*)
You heard the man. Go on outta here.

Foley doesn't move, just gives the guy a bored once-over.

MAURICE

Himey here's a pro-toh-jay of mine. He's ranked number thirty-two in the federal prison system.

FOLEY
(looking at Himey)
Thirty-two outta what, twenty?

Himey bulldozes forward, pulling his massive fist back to clock Foley in the head when . . .

In one swift motion Foley brings his book up in one hand, like he's throwing a pie, and drives the hefty repair manual into Himey's face, snapping the big guy's head back, sending his feet flying out from under him so that he hits the floor back-first with a loud thud.

Maurice goes for Foley, who picks up the chair just as we hear a whistle. They all freeze and look to a prisoner at another table, who nods towards the door.

We pan over just as a guard appears, takes in the scene as a dazed Himey slowly pulls himself up, covers his now bleeding nose.

GUARD

What's going on here?

MAURICE

Oh, you know, reading's funnamental an' shit, we just excited.

GUARD

Clear outta here.

The guard exits. Maurice and Foley are still staring at each other.

RIPLEY

Excuse me. Snoopy? Did we settle the fish thing?

MAURICE
(looks at Foley)
Yeah. Sure. It's all settled.

*He pours the water out of the bag and drops the fish into
Ripley's open hand. Maurice then squeezes Ripley's hand into a
fist, crushing the fish. He taps his fist to Ripley's.*

> RIPLEY

That's how you do it.

*Maurice gives Foley a last look, starts out of the room with
Himey. Ripley looks at the crushed fish in his hand, then at
Foley.*

> RIPLEY

Thanks for your help.

> FOLEY

Any time.

We hear a phone ring and then . . .

CUT TO:

MAURICE MILLER'S HOUSE. THE BEDROOM (NOW)

Maurice lies in bed watching a boxing match on television.

> MAURICE

Stick and jab, fool. Stick and jab.

*A frisbee whizzes past the television. We hear a dog yelp off-
screen.*

Hey! Watch that shit!

*Maurice's girlfriend, Moselle – about thirty, sleepy-eyed, in a
green bathrobe – picks the frisbee up off the floor as the phone
rings away on the bedside table right next to Maurice.*

> MOSELLE
> *(calls off-screen)*

Tuffy. C'mere, boy . . .

> MAURICE

You gonna answer the phone?

What for? It's not for me.

Maurice watches as Moselle now tries to throw the frisbee to a little wire-haired terrier, but it just bounces off the dog's head.

Bad dog.

MAURICE
(*scoops up the dog*)
Moselle, the fuck are you doing to my little Tuffy?

He lovingly nuzzles the dog like it's his child.

MOSELLE

I'm trainin' Tuffy, so he can be on a Kal Kan commercial, make us some extra money.

He looks at her.

MAURICE

That's the dumbest thing I heard in my life. Everybody knows Kal Kan doesn't pay for shit. You gonna get a gig, it's gotta be for one of the big three: Science Diet, Iams or that Cycle shit for the fat dogs. Now answer the fuckin' phone.

She comes over, picks up the phone.

MOSELLE

Hello?
(*hands it to Maurice*)
For you.

MAURICE
(*takes it*)
This is me.

EXT. PHONE BOOTH. GAS STATION. NIGHT

An antsy Glenn with his shades on talks on the phone.

GLENN

Snoopy. Glenn Michaels.

Intercutting Glenn and Maurice:

> MAURICE

Studs. Hey, son, you must be one a them psychic friends. I was just thinkin' about you.

Glenn watches as some guy in a suit gets out of a black Lincoln Town Car and jogs to the john.

> GLENN

Listen, Snoopy, I'm on my way up to Detroit and need a place to crash.

> MAURICE

You crazy, come up *here*? It's fuckin' one degree outside.

> GLENN

I wanna talk to you about a job.

> MAURICE

Uh-huh.

> GLENN

I can't really go into it right now. I'll just tell you it's someone big.

> MAURICE

Some*one*? Gimme a hint.

> GLENN

It's a guy you know.

> MAURICE

Gimme another hint.

> GLENN

It's Richard Ripley.

Maurice doesn't say a word.

You there?

> MAURICE

Oh, I'm here, all right. I'm very here. Question is, why aren't *you* here?

EXT. BUDDY'S APARTMENT. SOMEWHERE IN FLORIDA. NIGHT

As Foley and Buddy hurry up the front steps.

FOLEY

I'm just saying she wasn't scared.

BUDDY

'Cause she had her hand on her gun the whole time, waiting
to make her move.

Buddy opens the door, looks at Foley.

FOLEY

You're just jealous it was me in the trunk with her and not
you.

BUDDY

You're right.

INT. BUDDY'S APARTMENT. NIGHT

*A 'hideout'. Not much in the way of furnishings. Foley follows
Buddy inside, watches as he bolts the door.*

FOLEY

First thing I'm gonna do is get all this mud off me.

Foley starts for the bathroom.

I've been dreaming about a hot bath for the last six months.
Soak the prison off me.

BUDDY

There's some lilac oil, you want some, a vanilla candle under
the sink.

FOLEY

Oh, man.

BUDDY

There's something about a nice hot bath, transforms a
person. It's not just about opening up your pores, know
what I mean? There's just something about the heat and the

wet that's calming, you know? Settles me in a way that I really can't articulate.

> FOLEY
> I know exactly what you mean. It's just a feeling.
> (*beat*)
> You know, I could go for some wine tonight.

> BUDDY
> There's a store around the corner, I'll be right back.

> FOLEY
> Sounds great.

Foley goes into the bathroom. A moment later we hear the bath running.

INT. APARTMENT HALLWAY. DAY

As Buddy leaves the apartment, starts down the hall, Karen steps into frame, watches as he disappears down the stairs. Gun drawn, she then moves towards the apartment.

INT. BATHROOM. DAY

As Foley undresses, picks up a candle off the sink and smells it. He notices his nude image in the mirror and checks himself out.

INT. APARTMENT. DAY

As Karen slips the door. She looks around, hears the water running.

She racks the slide on her gun, snicks off the safety and starts for the bathroom. Suddenly, the water is turned off. She stops where she is. She then moves a careful step at a time towards the open doorway.

Gradually the tub comes into view, beginning with Foley's feet resting crossed on the other end, then the middle of the tub, then she's in the doorway, looking down at . . .

Foley, lying there in the tub, his eyes closed. Karen cuts her eyes

*down the length of him, taking a moment here to check him out,
long enough for Foley to open his eyes and grab her hand, the
one holding the gun.*

> FOLEY

Hey.

*They look at each other a moment. He then pulls her down to
him and kisses her. She kisses him back. He then pulls her into
the tub with him as we now hear . . .*

> MARSHALL SISCO
> (*voice-over*)

Karen . . . ?

CUT TO:

Karen as she opens her eyes.

> KAREN

What?

INT. HOSPITAL ROOM. DAY

*Flowers everywhere. Karen – bruises on her face – lies in bed.
Her father, Marshall, sits on the chair beside her.*

> MARSHALL

You were talking in your sleep.

> KAREN
> (*beat*)

What'd I say?

> MARSHALL

'Hey, yourself.'

> KAREN

Huh.

*We hear a knock at the door. They look to where Special Agent
Daniel Burdon – black, forties, expensive suit – stands in the
doorway, file in one hand.*

KAREN

Hello, Daniel.

BURDON
(to Marshall)

Daniel Burdon, FBI.

MARSHALL

Marshall Sisco. Karen's dad.

BURDON

You mind please waiting outside. We have some business to do here.

Marshall looks at him a moment. Then, to Karen . . .

MARSHALL

I need to go to the john anyway.

Burdon waits for Marshall to walk out, then sits down.

KAREN

I wanna be on the task force, Daniel.

BURDON

That's nice of you to offer, Karen, but I got all the help I can use right now. Instead, let's talk about how you got the bump on your head.

KAREN
(indicates file)

Isn't that my report you're holding on to?

BURDON

Yes, but I want to hear you tell it. Starting with when you tried to grab the wheel – where was this?

KAREN

Coming to the Okeechobee exit . . .

And now we see it . . .

IN THE CAR

Going over a hundred miles per hour, blowing past cars . . .

>   KAREN
>
> Take the next exit.

>   GLENN
>
> What am I supposed to do *now*?

>   KAREN
>
> Glenn, take the exit.

>   GLENN
>
> No way, man, no fuckin' way am I gonna turn myself in.

She reaches over and grabs the wheel.

> The fuck are you doing?!

He hits the brakes. The car goes off the road, down the slope, the abutment coming right at us as we go back to . . .

THE HOSPITAL ROOM

Burdon sets the file down, sits back now.

>   KAREN
>
> The next thing I knew, the paramedics were taking me out of the car.

Burdon looks at Karen a moment, then . . .

>   BURDON
>
> There's a couple of points I keep wondering about to do with the two guys that grabbed you. Buddy, is it? And this fella Jack Foley. I swear the man must've robbed two hundred banks in his time.

>   KAREN
>
> Really? Huh. He told me he didn't remember how many he robbed.

>   BURDON
>
> You talked to him?

KAREN

In the trunk, yeah?

BURDON

What'd you talk about?

KAREN

Oh . . . different things, prison, movies.

BURDON

This fella holds you hostage, you talk about movies?

KAREN

It was an unusual experience.

BURDON

Foley made me think of that fella Carl Tillman, the one you were seeing, it turns out the same time he was doing banks. You recall that?

KAREN

When I was seeing Carl Tillman, I didn't know he robbed banks.

BURDON

Yeah, but I had enough reason to believe he did, and I told you. So you had to at least suspect him.

KAREN

And what happened to Carl?

BURDON

The time came, you shot him. But you didn't shoot Foley or the guy with him. They're unarmed, you had a shotgun and you let them throw you in the trunk. OK, now you got your Sig in your hand. You say in the report you couldn't turn around, he had you pinned down. But when the trunk opened, how come you didn't cap the two guys then?

KAREN

Is that what you would've done?

BURDON

You say in the report Glenn didn't have a gun, but you let him get away, too.

KAREN

Daniel, what do you work on most of the time, fraud? Go after crooked book-keepers.

BURDON

Karen, I've been with the Bureau fifteen years, on all kinds of investigations.

KAREN

Have you ever shot a man? How many times have you been primary through the door?

BURDON

I have to qualify, is that it?

KAREN

You have to know what you're talking about.

We hear chuckling off-screen. Burdon glances at the doorway, where we see Marshall now standing, enjoying this.

BURDON

We'll talk another time, Karen. All right? I'd like to know why Foley put you in that second car when he didn't need you any more.

KAREN

You'll have to ask him.

BURDON

Sounds to me like he liked having you around. I'll see you, Karen. Mr Sisco.

MARSHALL

Agent Burdon.

Marshall waits for him to walk out.

The white man's Burdon. That's what everybody calls him in

Miami. The Metro-Dade guys. He's got a knack for pissing people off.

She's not listening. He sits down, takes her hand.

What are you thinking about?

KAREN
The Sig-Sauer you got me for my birthday.

MARSHALL
Tell you what, you're a good girl, you might get another one for Christmas.

She looks at him.

KAREN
I'll get it back when I get Foley.

EXT. BUDDY'S APARTMENT BUILDING. DAY

A dozen geriatric residents sit on chairs out front as Buddy climbs the steps carrying a bag of groceries under one arm, newspaper under the other. An old woman comes out the door as Buddy opens it and squints at him.

OLD WOMAN
Oh – are you delivering the oxygen?

BUDDY
Uh, no, ma'am. Sorry.

INT. BUDDY'S APARTMENT. DAY

Buddy's real apartment, not the one Karen pictured in her dream. This one's nicer, with a view of the beach. Jack stands on the balcony going through Karen's bag.

He pulls out her wallet, checks out her driver's licence photo. He does the same with her gym ID card. He finds her address book and opens it up. A photo of her father slips out. Jack examines it a moment, then flips through the book.

He stares at something in her bag a moment, then reaches in and comes up with her US Marshal ID. He slips it open and studies the badge and the picture opposite.

He holds on to it, looks out at the ocean, but really sees . . .

THE OPEN TRUNK OF THE CAR — LAST NIGHT

As Karen gets out, saying . . .

> KAREN
>
> You win, Jack.

INT. BUDDY'S APARTMENT. DAY

Foley turns away from the view as Buddy walks in, sets the grocery bag down on the coffee table.

> BUDDY
>
> You made the front page.

He holds up the newspaper so that Foley can see his picture on the front page: an unflattering mug shot that doesn't look all that much like him.

> They pass this picture around you can go anywhere you want, nobody'll know you.

> FOLEY
>
> I wasn't feeling my best that day. I'd just drawn thirty to life.

> BUDDY
>
> Maybe this'll make you feel better.

Buddy reaches into the bag, tosses Foley a new Zippo.

> FOLEY
>
> Thanks.

Foley catches the lighter, immediately begins playing with it. He looks at the paper on the coffee table as Buddy sits down, pulls some groceries and a six-pack from the bag.

> BUDDY
>
> Paper says there's ten grand each on you, Chino and Lulu.

FOLEY

Say anything in there about Karen Sisco?

BUDDY

Just that she got away.

FOLEY

Yeah, but what happened after she drove off with Glenn?

BUDDY

You'll have to ask Glenn. And most likely, he's on his way to Detroit, where we should be.

Foley walks back out on to the balcony, looks at the contents of Karen's bag spread out on the table.

You realize what you're doing? Worrying about a person that works in law enforcement. You want to sit down and have cocktails with a girl that tried to shoot you. You hear what I'm saying?

Foley holds up the picture of Marshall Sisco.

FOLEY

Think this old guy is her boyfriend? It's the only picture she carries.

BUDDY

Am I going to Detroit by myself?

Foley picks up her driver's licence photo.

Longer we hang around down here, Jack, better chance there is either Glenn's gonna fuck up the whole score, or we gonna get busted, or both.

FOLEY

We'll leave first thing in the morning.

EXT. MARSHALL SISCO'S CONDO. DAY

Right on a marina. Boats bobbing on the water.

(*voice-over*)

Is *this* Foley?

INT. MARSHALL SISCO'S CONDO. DAY

Marshall sits in his chair holding up a newspaper as Karen hands him a drink. She stares at the photograph.

KAREN

He doesn't even look like that.

MARSHALL

No?

KAREN

No, he looks a lot . . .

She realizes Marshall's watching her.

Different.

The doorbell rings. She ignores his look, gets up. Walks to the door and opens it to reveal Ray Nicolet – boots, leather jacket, etc. Cowboy Cop.

Hi, Ray.

RAY

You look great. Your dad taking good care of you?

KAREN

He took the week off so we'd have time together. So far he's worked on his boat every day. Dad? Ray Nicolet.

Marshall gets up, shakes his head.

RAY

I've heard a lot about you, Mr Sisco.

MARSHALL

Likewise.

KAREN

Ray's with the FBI Task Force, working on the prison break.

MARSHALL
(*eyeing his T-shirt*)

I see that.

Ray turns to Karen, holding his jacket open to show the Task Force inscription on his T-shirt in red. The guy's .357 is tucked into his waistband.

In case no one knows what he does. Tell me, Ray, you ever wear one says, 'Undercover'?

RAY

No. 'Course not.

KAREN
(*changing the subject*)

How's it going?

RAY

Great. We got one of 'em.

Karen looks at him.

KAREN

Was it Foley?

MARSHALL
(*before he can answer*)

Off a tip?

RAY

Yeah, someone spotted two of 'em in this hobo camp out by the airport, called the number –

MARSHALL

I knew it, soon as I saw they were offering a reward.

She grabs Nicolet by the arm.

KAREN

Was it Foley?

Marshall looks at her.

RAY

Foley? Oh. No, it was one of the Cubans. Linares.

KAREN

Oh . . .

RAY

We went out there, full SWAT, two choppers, the whole bit, but Linares started shooting anyway. We put him down, but somehow Chirino got away.

MARSHALL

Did you pay the guy the reward?

RAY

Yeah, as soon as we got back.

KAREN

Foley hadn't been there?

Her father gives her a look.

RAY

This place was strictly Cuban. If Foley had a ride he must have his own agenda. He seems to be the only one knows what he's doing.

The phone rings. Marshall moves to it.

MARSHALL

Hello?
                    (*beat*)
Yeah, she is. Just a minute.
                    (*hands her the phone*)
For you.

KAREN

Hello?

CUT TO:

Foley on the phone. On the balcony. Flipping through a copy of Vogue *while Buddy watches television inside.*

FOLEY

Hi.

Intercutting Karen and Foley:

Karen just stands there, sees her father looking at her as Ray drones on.

You know who this is?

KAREN

Yes.

She walks out to her father's balcony now.

FOLEY

I just wanted to see if you're OK, make sure Glenn didn't hurt you or, you know, anything.

MARSHALL

Something I've been wondering, Ray . . .

Marshall picks up the newspaper . . .

It says in the headline, '"I slept with a murderer," says shaken Miami woman.' She lives in Little Havana, her husband's out of town working when one of the escapees shows up at her door.

She closes the glass door, so that they won't hear her.

KAREN

How'd you get this number?

FOLEY

Who was it answered the phone?

KAREN

None of your business.

FOLEY

I'm just worried maybe I'm not old enough for you.

KAREN

That's my dad.

FOLEY

Really. He has a cop's face.

KAREN

How do you know? Wait – you have my wallet.

FOLEY

And your gun.

KAREN

Think I could have them back?

FOLEY

How do we do that?

KAREN

Let's see. You could come on by my dad's place, drop 'em off.

FOLEY

Sure. I'll just leave 'em with the SWAT guy answers the door.

Foley stops flipping through the magazine, stares at what he's been looking for: an ad for Defiance perfume.

KAREN

There's a guy here on the Task Force right now. Maybe I should put him on the phone, let you two work it out.

FOLEY

You won't do that.

KAREN

Why not?

FOLEY

Because you're having too much fun.

She doesn't know what to say to that. Foley smells the ad.

Inside the house . . .

MARSHALL

. . . She fixes him pork chops and rice, the next thing you know they're making love on the sofa. She says he was very gentle.

64

RAY

I spoke to her. The guy told her he missed his little girl and she felt sorry for him.

MARSHALL

That's how you score now?

On the patio, Karen looks inside at her father talking with Ray Nicolet.

KAREN

My dad's retired. He was a private investigator. Forty years. I used to work for him.

FOLEY

I can just picture that, a cute girl like you following slip-and-fall and whiplash cheaters.

KAREN

Something I've been wondering, whatever happened to your Uncle Cully?

FOLEY

Why? You think he might tell you where I am?

KAREN

Unless you wanna tell me.

FOLEY

He's dead. He did twenty-seven years before he came out and died not too long after in Charity Hospital, I think trying to make up for all the good times he'd missed.
(*pause*)
That's not gonna be me.

KAREN

One last score, that the idea? Move to some island.

FOLEY

I'm partial to mountains myself. But if you like islands, we'll make it an island.

                                KAREN
Whatta you mean *we'll* make it an island?

                                FOLEY
I just thought maybe you and me could –

Buddy opens the door, sticks his head out, startles Foley.

                                BUDDY
Who you talking to?

                                KAREN
Is that Buddy?

*Foley's caught off-guard, hangs up the phone. He looks at
Buddy.*

                                FOLEY
What?!

                                BUDDY
You better come see this.

INT. MARSHALL'S CONDO. DAY

*Karen stands on the balcony another moment, then hangs up,
opens the sliding door and walks back into the living room.*

                                RAY
The woman also said he stole her husband's gun, a .22
pistol, and some of his clothes.

                                MARSHALL
So the woman's married. She goes to bed with this prison
escapee because he misses his little girl and then tells the
world about it. But you don't reveal her name, you protect
her. It sounds like you're saying it's OK as long as her
husband doesn't find out about it. Like the guy who cheats
on his wife, saying what she doesn't know won't hurt her.

                                KAREN
Dad.

He looks over at her now. Gives her an innocent look.

What?

INT. BUDDY'S APARTMENT. DAY

As Foley and Buddy watch a news report on the earlier events at the hobo camp. We catch a glimpse of Ray Nicolet, gun in his waistband, sticking his chest out for the camera.

Foley shakes his head as they show a shot of Lulu's body covered with a sheet.

FOLEY

Chino's gonna wanna talk to me.

BUDDY

He's running for his life, he doesn't give a shit about you.

FOLEY

He's gotta know by now that I gave him up back at Glades. He does, he's gonna try to find me. Maybe go see Adele, see what she knows.

BUDDY

He knows where she lives?

Foley doesn't answer. Buddy mutes the set. Turns to Foley.

Jack?

FOLEY

We were talking one time, drinking rum. I may've mentioned Adele, how she worked for a magician. Chino got interested. He's like, Yeah? How does he saw the woman in half? He wanted to meet her. Or get a look at her if she ever came to visit.

BUDDY

So call her up. Tell her don't talk to any Cubans.

FOLEY

Her phone's probably tapped.

And you know they're gonna have some people watching
the hotel.

FOLEY

Shit.

EXT. MARSHALL SISCO'S BOAT. DAY

*Karen stands there with her car keys and bag as Marshall paints
the trim on the boat.*

MARSHALL

Remember, pay attention to how she talks about Foley, her
tone. Do it right, she'll tell you things she wouldn't tell
Burdon. Tell her you think he's a nice guy. No, first tell her
about being in the trunk with him, in the dark for half an
hour, and see how she takes it. If she's in on it, what does
she get for all the aggravation: cops breathing on her? I bet
nothing. So she still likes him enough to stick her neck out.
You think that's possible? What kind of guy is he?

KAREN

He's pretty laid-back, confident.

MARSHALL

He remind you of that guy, Tillman?

KAREN

Not at all.

MARSHALL

But you know he's dirty and you still wanna see him again.

KAREN

I want to bust his ass, put him in shackles.

MARSHALL

Maybe. But you're also curious about the man. Twice last
night you asked your married boyfriend Nicolet about him.
You were concerned, but you didn't want to show it.

KAREN

My married boyfriend – setting him up with that news story so you could talk about infidelity. I couldn't believe it.

MARSHALL

You like the wild ones, don't you? Tillman, Nicolet and now Foley. You know, I've always said there's a thin line between the cowboy cops and the armed robbers, all those guys that love to pack.

KAREN

Foley *kid*napped me.

MARSHALL

Yeah, but you talked all the way from GCI to the turnpike. It sounds more like a first date than a kidnapping.

She gives him a look. He goes back to his painting.

Go talk to the ex-wife.

INT. ADELE DELISI'S APARTMENT. DAY

Adele comes in, drops a stack of her cards on the glass-topped dining table and turns on the window air-conditioner when the phone rings. She grabs it.

ADELE

Hi, this is Adele speaking.

EXT. PAY PHONE. DAY

Adele's neighbourhood. Near the beach. Chino on the phone. He wears a painter's cap and a white jumpsuit.

CHINO

Oh, is this Adele?

ADELE
(*phone*)

Yes, it is.

CHINO

Uh – sorry. Wrong number.

He hangs up, glances about, then checks the little .22 stuck in one of his pockets. As he then starts off down the street, we can see the name 'COLOUR MY WORLD HOUSEPAINTING' on the back of the jumpsuit.

INT. BUDDY'S CAR. DAY

Buddy drives. Foley – in a bright orange and ochre beach outfit – is beside him. Buddy looks at him, shakes his head.

BUDDY

Nice disguise.

FOLEY

I'm a tourist.

BUDDY

You at least bring the gun?

FOLEY
(*lifts straw bag*)
In here with my suntan lotion and beach towel.
(*points*)
That's her place.

As they drive past, Buddy indicates a man on the steps out front, obviously FBI.

BUDDY

There. You see the guy sitting on the porch? The old ladies and one guy? You know they'll have a couple more in a car somewhere.

FOLEY
(*watching something else*)
Uh-huh . . .

Buddy follows Foley's gaze across the street.

A car door opens and Karen Sisco gets out, rifling in her bag for change. She drops a quarter. Foley is now watching as she bends down to grab it, her skirt hiking way up her thigh.

> BUDDY
>
> Oh, my.

Foley watches, her hair in her face as she tries to reach under the car and grab it.

> OK, you saw her. That's all you get.

They watch as she walks to the Normandie and shows the Young Agent her ID . . .

> FOLEY
>
> I guess Adele's in good hands.

> BUDDY
>
> Sure looks that way.

> FOLEY
> (*finally*)
>
> Let's go to Detroit.

> BUDDY
>
> Now you're talkin'.

INT. HALLWAY OUTSIDE ADELE'S APARTMENT. DAY

Adele has the chain on the door, talks to Karen through the narrow opening.

> ADELE
>
> You were *both* in the trunk? Together?

> KAREN
>
> From Glades to the turnpike. Then I left with Glenn.

Karen watches Adele's face in the opening, freshly made-up, heavy on the eyeshadow and lip gloss.

> The FBI didn't tell you I was with them?

> ADELE
>
> They didn't *tell* me anything, they asked questions.

KAREN

But you know what I'm talking about, don't you? About Glenn, don't you, and the second car?

ADELE

I know a Glenn.

She thinks a moment. The door closes and opens again, all the way. Adele stands there in a robe, hanging partly open, panties, but no bra.

I'm getting ready to go out. You can come in if you want, sit down for a minute. Would you like a Diet Coke?

KAREN

No, thanks.

She comes in, checks out the place. She turns a chair from the glass-top table and sits down as Adele comes out of the kitchenette with a Diet Coke and packet of cigarettes.

ADELE

Those are cute shoes. The kind of jobs I get, I have to wear these killer spikes, they ruin your feet.

She walks away, comes back with an ashtray.

When you were in the trunk with Jack . . .

Karen waits, watches her light her cigarette.

He didn't hurt you or anything, did he?

KAREN

You mean, did he try to jump me? No, but he was kind of talkative.

ADELE

He gets that way when he's nervous sometimes.

Adele sits down at the other end of the table.

KAREN

You didn't visit him in prison.

ADELE

He didn't want me to.

KAREN

Why not?

ADELE

I don't know. He was different after he was sentenced, looking at thirty years. Said it depressed him every time the younger cons called him an old-timer.

KAREN

But you spoke to him on the phone.

ADELE

He'd call every once in a while.

KAREN

He called the day he escaped.

ADELE

He did? I don't remember. Did he say about me? In the trunk?

KAREN
(*beat, lies*)

He said he wished the two of you could start over, live a normal life.

ADELE

Huh. Problem is, Jack's idea of a normal life is robbing banks. It's all he's ever done.

KAREN

Did you know that when you married him?

ADELE

He said he was a card player. I could live with that. I never knew he robbed banks till he got busted with that car that caught fire – if you can imagine something like that happening, comes out of the bank and the car's on fire. I did go see him in jail to tell him I was filing for divorce. He said, 'OK.' Jack's so easygoing.

(pause)

He was fun, but never what you'd call a real husband.

Adele looks out the window. Karen waits, looks to an end table where she sees a photograph of Jack and Adele on a boat somewhere ten years back.

I'll say one thing for Jack, he was never ugly or mean, or drank too much. He was very considerate, lights on or off, if you know what I mean.

KAREN

Really.
(looking at the picture)
Hm.

She realizes Adele is looking at her.

Adele, sooner or later, he's gonna get caught. I'd like to get him before he does something else, makes it worse on himself.

ADELE

Buddy'll take care of him. Keep him out've trouble. He's Jack's conscience. Always has been.
(chuckles)
He tell you how they met?

Karen shakes her head.

Jack came out of a bank he just robbed in Pasadena, couldn't get his stolen car to start. Battery was dead. He looks over, sees Buddy sitting in a burgundy Bonneville, goes up, offers him a thousand dollars for a jump. Turns out, Buddy was casing the same bank and saw the whole thing. Buddy says, I'll take the thousand, but we're leaving in my car, not that piece of shit you come in.
(pause)
They musta robbed fifty banks together.

KAREN

Till they got busted.

74

ADELE

That wasn't Jack's fault. No, that was on account of Buddy,
for some reason, decided to call his sister and confess to a
job *before* they'd done it instead of after. She called the FBI
and they both went down, ended up at Lompoc.

(*pause*)

I think Buddy felt kinda bad about that.

KAREN

Any idea where I could find Buddy? Or Glenn?

*Adele looks at Karen, then jumps at the sound of three quick
raps on the door.*

CHINO'S VOICE

Adele? You in there?

ADELE

Yes.

CHINO

I want to speak with you, please.

ADELE

Who is it?

CHINO'S VOICE

I talk to the guy you work for, Emil. He tole me your
number and where you live. See, I'm looking for an assistant
and would like to speak to you.

ADELE

Oh. Uh-huh.

CHINO'S VOICE

You did work for Emil, right?

ADELE

Yeah, I was Emil's box-jumper for almost four years.

CHINO'S VOICE

You were his what, his box?

His assistant.

Karen looks at the door. Something's wrong . . . Through the glass bricks that line one side of the door, we see blurred movement on the other side, someone doing something . . .

You say you perform in the Miami area?

CHINO'S VOICE
Yes, around here. I was a mayishan in Cuba before I come here. Manuel the Mayishan was my name.

And now Karen and Adele look at each other.

Can you open the door?

Karen shakes her head 'no'.

ADELE
I'm not dressed.

CHINO'S VOICE
Listen to me.
(*lowers his voice*)
I'm a good friend of Jack Foley.

Boom. Karen gets to her feet, brings her bag to the edge of the table, sees Adele staring at her.

KAREN
Ask him his name.

ADELE
Who are you?

CHINO'S VOICE
(*beat*)
José Chirino.

Karen brings her Beretta out of the bag.

Or maybe you hear Jack Foley call me Chino. I'm the same person.

76

Karen moves along the table to Adele.

> KAREN
> (*soft*)
>
> Tell him to wait in the hall, you have to get dressed. Say it loud.

As Adele speaks, Karen racks the slide on her 9mm.

> ADELE
>
> Wait in the hall! I have to get dressed!

> CHINO'S VOICE
>
> Tell me where is Jack Foley, I don't bother you no more.

Karen motions for Adele to keep talking as she takes a position beside the door, where we now see Chino's silhouette in one of the three glass panels in the centre of the door.

> ADELE
>
> I don't know where he is.

> CHINO'S VOICE
>
> Listen, I'm the one help Jack escape from prison. He tole me, I can't find him to see you. So why don't you open this fucking door. OK? So we can speak.

> ADELE
> (*staring at Karen*)
>
> Go away, or I'll call the police.

> CHINO'S VOICE
>
> Why you want to do that, to a frien'?

Adele says nothing. Then . . .

> OK, you don't want to help me, I'm leaving.
> (*pause*)
> I'm going now. I see you maybe some time, OK? Bye-bye.

> KAREN
> (*low*)
>
> Go in the bedroom and –

Suddenly, Chino's fist – wrapped in his shirt – explodes through one of the glass panels. Adele and Karen both jump as Chino pushes his arm through, reaches for the doorknob . . .

But Karen grabs the knob first and, using all of her weight as leverage, pivots and flings the door open with Chino's arm still sticking through the glass . . .

The force of this slingshots the man into the room, where he bangs against a wall and falls to the floor. Dazed, Chino reaches for his .22 as he now tries to get to his feet.

Karen brings up her Beretta in two hands, cocks it and puts the front sight on his chest.

Leave it where it is.

CHINO
(*frowning*)
Wait. You not Adele?

KAREN
I'm a federal marshal and you're under arrest. Put the gun on the table. I mean, now.

CHINO
Oh. Then this must be Adele . . .

He now aims the gun point-blank at Adele.

KAREN
Put it down or I'll shoot.

CHINO
You wouldn't shoot me, would you?

KAREN
What do you want to bet?

CHINO
(*beat*)
I could walk out of here.

KAREN

If you move, if you look at her again, you're dead.

Chino doesn't move. Keeps his gun on Adele. Karen starts walking towards him.

You can live or die, it's up to you.

CHINO

Oh, is that right? You going to shoot me? Nice girl like you?
(*smiles*)
I don't think so.

KAREN

You don't, huh?

And with that, she kicks him in the knee. Chino buckles over and she hits him on the side of the head with her gun.

On your knees.

He does as he's told. Karen raises his jacket, feels around his waist from behind.

Lie face down on the floor.

CHINO
(*hurting*)

What?!

She kicks him over on to his stomach and stays there. She puts her foot to his back as she reaches for the phone, dials. She sees Adele staring at her.

(*to Adele*)
Excuse me . . .

Karen looks at Adele a moment, then says into the phone . . .

KAREN

Daniel Burdon, please. Karen Sisco.

CHINO

Excuse me, Adele?

ADELE

Yes.

CHINO

You do the sawing of the box in half trick with you inside?

ADELE
(*beat*)

Yes.

CHINO

Tell me, how do you do that?

Adele looks at Karen, who shoves Chino's head to the floor with her foot.

KAREN

Shut up.

BURDON
(*phone*)

Karen. Where are you? I been trying to get a hold of you.

KAREN

Daniel. Listen –

BURDON
(*phone*)

Where are you? I been trying to reach you.

KAREN

I'm at Adele Delisi's.

BURDON

What – we already talked to her. That's a dead end.

KAREN
(*looking at Chino*)

Yeah, I know. I was just leaving. Why were you trying to reach me?

BURDON

There was a Buddy Bragg at Lompoc around the same time Foley was there. We got an address for him at the Adams

Hotel in Hallandale. I want you to go there, see if you can get the manager to ID him as the other guy. If he does, you call me right away.

KAREN

All right, but . . .

BURDON
(*phone*)
But don't you *do* anything. You just have a seat, wait for me to get there.

KAREN

Sure, Daniel.

BURDON
(*phone*)
Now. What is it you wanted to tell me?

KAREN

Oh, I was just wondering, if I were to bring in Chirino, would you put me on the Task Force?

BURDON
(*phone, impatient*)
What? Is that what you're calling me about?

KAREN

Yes or no, Daniel. If I get him, will you let me go after Foley?

BURDON
(*phone*)
Yeah, sure, Karen. You bring in Chirino, you can be on the Task Force.

KAREN

That's all I wanted to know.

BURDON
(*phone*)
Good. Now forget about the ex-wife and get over to the Adams Hotel.

Karen hangs up, looks at Adele. Adele nods.

ADELE

You're good.

KAREN

Thank you.

INT. BUDDY'S APARTMENT. NIGHT

Foley and Buddy quickly pack up their stuff.

FOLEY

First thing we do, we get to Detroit, we find Glenn, then we find a window to throw him out of.

BUDDY

I been thinkin', if I was Glenn, I was up there to take down the Ripper, where would I go?

FOLEY

Well, first off, if you were Glenn, you wouldn't be thinking.

BUDDY

Remember Snoopy Miller, his old pal from Lompoc?

FOLEY

Snoopy. Christ, I thought he'd be brain-dead by now.

BUDDY

He isn't fighting no more. Glenn told me the Snoop's been managing some guys up there now, works out at the Kronk.

INT. SHALAMAR APARTMENTS. LOBBY. NIGHT

The ancient residents stop what they're doing as Burdon enters with eight guys in jackets and wool shirts hanging out, running shoes, half of them carrying what look like athletic bags. Karen meets them as they all walk to the elevator.

BURDON

You get the key?

KAREN

They're in 7D.

She hands it to him as they wait for the elevator.

BURDON

I want two men outside, front and back. Conway and Jessup go on up to seven, cover both ends of the hall.

Burdon, Karen and the remaining four SWAT team agents. Burdon looks at them one at a time.

You're primary, you're secondary, you're point man.

KAREN

You're gonna use a ram?

BURDON

Yeah, why?

KAREN

The manager's door is metal.

They all look at her.

You know what I mean? They might all be. And a ram on a metal door makes an awful lot of noise for what good it does.

Burdon looks at her, not all that happy she spoke up. The fourth man raises the shotgun, a three-inch strip of metal taped to the muzzle.

FOURTH MAN

I got a shock-lock round in my shotgun oughta do the trick.

BURDON

Fine. Whatever.

He sees the elevator still hasn't come down.

Fuck it. Let's take the stairs. Karen . . .

Burdon pauses, looks at Karen, hands her a radio.

Take the radio, stay down here in the lobby, watch the elevator.

KAREN

What? Daniel, I wanna go upstairs.

BURDON

You can go wait out in the car, you want to.

She doesn't say anything.

Now you see Foley and this guy Bragg come in behind us, whatta you do?

KAREN
(*angry*)

Call and tell you.

BURDON

And you let them come up. You don't try to make the bust yourself. You understand?

Before she can answer, an old woman steps in, asks Burdon . . .

OLD WOMAN

Are you delivering the oxygen?

Burdon looks at her, then nods for his men to start up the stairs.

INT. THE SEVENTH FLOOR. DAY

Everyone's in position as Burdon eases the key into the lock, turns it. The door won't budge, a dead bolt holds it shut.

The guy with the shotgun puts the strip of metal against the seam, where the lock enters the frame, the muzzle of the shotgun exactly three inches now from the dead bolt, and looks over his shoulder at Burdon.

With the sound of the blast, we then . . .

CUT TO:

INT. ELEVATOR. DAY

Foley and Buddy ride down with an old lady. The doors open. The woman doesn't move.

84

BUDDY

Is this your floor, mother?

OLD LADY

Oh. Yes, it is.

INT. LOBBY. DAY

An old gent in a golf cap smiles at Karen sitting there on the couch in front of the elevator.

OLD GENT

Like to play some gin?

KAREN

No, thank you.

He creeps off towards the elevator.

INT. BUDDY'S APARTMENT. DAY

Burdon and his men fan out through the place.

INT. LOBBY. DAY

We hear Burdon's voice.

BURDON
(*radio*)

Karen. They're not up here. Keep your eyes open.

Karen looks off towards the street entrance, then back at the elevator where the man is still waiting, leaning on his cane.

The elevator door opens to reveal Buddy and Foley.

OLD GENT

Going up?

Buddy and Foley don't answer. The old man starts to get on, feeling with his cane, taking for ever.

Karen and Foley are staring at each other. He doesn't move. Not until the elevator door begins to close.

Buddy sees Karen, helps the old man aboard as . . .

Karen picks up her radio, is about to speak into it when . . .

Foley raises his hand. And waves as the door closes.

INT. ELEVATOR. DAY

The elevator resumes going down.

> OLD GENT
> Shit, I wanted to go up.

> BUDDY
> Let's just hope there's no one in the garage.

> FOLEY
> She looked right at me. She didn't yell or get excited. She
> didn't move.

INT. BUDDY'S CAR. DAY

They get in and Buddy starts the car.

> BUDDY
> They know where I live, I guess they know what I drive, so
> maybe we should pick up another car on the way.

> FOLEY
> She just sat there, looking right at me.

*Buddy gives him a look, shakes his head and then burns rubber
out of the garage as we . . .*

CUT TO:

Close-up of Karen staring straight ahead.

> BURDON
> (*on the radio*)
> Karen. Report. You see anything? Karen? You there?
> Karen . . . ?

INT. AIRPORT TERMINAL. DAY

As Marshall walks Karen to the gate.

> MARSHALL

He waved to you?

> KAREN

I couldn't swear to it, but I'm pretty sure he did.

> MARSHALL

You wave back?

> KAREN

I didn't have time.

> MARSHALL

I imagine you would've though.

She shakes her head.

> KAREN

Buddy's sister Regina Mary Bragg got two calls from Buddy
up in Detroit this morning, called Burdon. She's also the one
gave Burdon Buddy's address.

> MARSHALL

So?

> KAREN

So what I want to know is why Buddy still calls his sister
every week even after she turned him in.

> MARSHALL

He doesn't seem to hold a grudge.
> *(pause)*
What *I* want to know is why, they got such a big score up
north, did Foley hang around Miami for so long?
> *(looks at her)*
Any thoughts on that one?

> KAREN

None I'd like to share.

She gives him a kiss

I'll call soon as I get in.

DISSOLVE TO:

EXT. BLOOMFIELD HILLS. DETROIT. DAY

Snow. Everywhere. A black Lincoln Town Car creeps through the neighbourhood full of big, beautiful snow-covered homes.

> MAURICE
> (*voice-over*)
> I don't just manage fighters, or deal product any more . . .

INT. CAR. DAY

Glenn – sunglasses – sits in the back with Maurice, a.k.a. 'Snoopy' – wearing a purple bandanna and his own dark sunglasses.

> MAURICE
> I've diversified since the last time you saw me. I've vertically integrated and now I'm into home invasions and the occasional grand larceny.

Glenn just nods, stares out the window.

> White Boy Bob's my all-around man, my bodyguard when I feel I need one, and my driver.

Maurice indicates White Boy Bob, a fucking huge, depraved-looking white guy now squeezed in behind the wheel.

> Watch the road, boy.
> (*pause*)
> I like this Town Car. We can cruise the man's neighbourhood without getting the police or private security people on our ass.

> GLENN
> Sure, right, they see Bigfoot driving around a black guy wearing shades and a lavender fucking bandanna, no, they won't think anything of it.

88

MAURICE

It's lilac, man, the colour, and the style's made known by
Deion and other defensive backs in the pros. I could be one
of them living out here with doctors of my race and
basketball players. OK, here comes Mr Ripley's house up on
the left. Yeah. The brick wall. There's his drive, right there.

The car creeps past a huge Tudor-style country house.

You sure Foley and his pal aren't coming up here, do this
themself?

GLENN

If they're not busted now, they're gonna be.
(*pause*)
It's wide open.

EXT./INT. CAR. MAURICE'S SHITTY NEIGHBOURHOOD IN
DETROIT. LATER

*People on the street with vacant expressions watch as the black
Town Car moves past the broken-down homes, cars on blocks
and snow-covered trash.*

GLENN

So you still haven't said, how you wanna do it?

MAURICE

I'll show you, soon as I get one more guy I'm gonna need,
Moselle's brother, Kenneth. Along with White Boy there.

GLENN

What?

*The car pulls to the kerb and Kenneth – a wiry black man in a
bright yellow T-shirt and red baseball cap backward, always
seems to be high on some chemical or another – gets in.*

MAURICE

You get everything?

*Kenneth tosses a gym bag into the back seat. Glenn stares at it.
Something about the bag makes him uneasy. Maybe it's the*

hacksaw that sticks partially out of the opening.

Cool. Kenneth, this is the man I told you about, Glenn.

KENNETH
The one gonna help us rip off the rich guy?

MAURICE
That's right.

GLENN
Help *you* . . .

*White Boy Bob pulls out again. Glenn looks at the two psychos
in front, then turns to Maurice.*

Wait a minute. I'm letting *you* in on this, not all your
friends.

MAURICE
You just ask me how we gonna do it. That's what I'm here
for, tell you how. We the experts.

Glenn can't believe this is happening.

Thing I'm worried about is you.

GLENN
Me?

MAURICE
Yeah. If you can step up and actually do it. Understand?
'Stead of just talking the talk.

GLENN
Can I do what?

MAURICE
Walk in a house with me, do this cross-dressin' nigga named
Eddie Solomon I used to sell to been dealin' on his own.

GLENN
What – when?

MAURICE

Right now, son.

GLENN

I don't have to prove shit to you. The Ripley job is *my* job.
You're either in or you're not. You wanna pop some crack
dealer pissed you off, that's your problem, not mine.

MAURICE

Look, Glenn, I know you cool, but you don't have to give
me no tone of voice, OK? You don't like what I'm saying,
you can get out anywhere along here you want.

GLENN

I think you're forgetting, this is my car. I drove it up here.

MAURICE

Hey, shit, come on. I say I want this car, man, it's mine. You
go get yourself another one. I say I'm in on Ripley, I'm in,
with or without *your* ass. I say I want you to come along on
another job, see if you for real or not, guess what you gonna
do?

Glenn looks at Maurice, now ice-cold behind the shades.

WHITE BOY BOB

We're here.

*Glenn looks out the window as they pull up in front of a
decrepit-looking two-storey house. Maurice opens the gym bag,
passes the hacksaw and a hand axe up to White Boy Bob, a
sawn-off shotgun to Kenneth, and takes out a big .45 for himself.*

MAURICE

Let's go see Eddie.

Glenn hesitates, then slowly gets out of the car as we hear . . .

RIPLEY
(*voice-over*)
Must take balls, do what you do.

As Foley walks with Ripley across the yard.

> RIPLEY
>
> Tell me something. What's it like, walk in a bank with a gun, stick it up?

> FOLEY
>
> I don't know. I never used a gun.

> RIPLEY
>
> Really?

> FOLEY
>
> You'd be surprised what all you can get, you ask for it the right way.

> RIPLEY
> (*smiles*)
>
> You're the reason, Jack, I don't keep all my money in banks.

> FOLEY
>
> No? Where do you keep it, Dick?

Ripley smiles.

> I'm talking about all those uncut diamonds you told Glenn about.

> RIPLEY
> (*still smiling*)
>
> I know what you're talking about.

> FOLEY
>
> You're the one with balls, Dick, say something like that to someone like Glenn. Or maybe you just forgot where you were for a minute.

> RIPLEY
>
> Yeah, but who's gonna believe Glenn? I mean, do *you* believe Glenn?

FOLEY

Of course not.

RIPLEY

Plus, even it was true, he'd still have to figure out where I keep 'em.

FOLEY

Doesn't have to figure out shit. You *told* him you keep 'em at your house.

RIPLEY

(shrugs, big smile)

It's a big house.

Ripley sits down on one of the picnic tables, looks around the yard.

Tell me something, Jack, how much longer you in here?

FOLEY

Twenty-two months, three days, two hours. Why?

RIPLEY

I was just thinking that I could use a guy like you, someone knows how to ask for things the right way. I'm talkin' about when you're outta here. I mean, you can't rob banks for ever.

Foley looks at Ripley.

FOLEY

It's a little late for me.

RIPLEY

Hey, Jack? Bullshit. I didn't make my first million until I was forty-two. Forty-two. You really *want* to change, it's never too late.

FOLEY

I don't know. I'm not exactly the nine-to-five type.

RIPLEY

Who is? But then you gotta look at a job as more than just

work. You gotta look at it as peace of mind. As *security*, you know what I mean? I got offices in Detroit, Miami, Boston, take your pick.

FOLEY

My ex-wife's in Miami. It's nice down there.

RIPLEY

No need to decide now. Be like the fish. Let whatever happens happen.

FOLEY

The fish?

RIPLEY

Yeah, fish live in the present. They don't dwell on yesterday and they don't worry about tomorrow. Even when a big fish attacks a little fish, there's no neurosis involved. No guilt afterward. No whining on some fish-shrink's couch. They just do it. They accept.

FOLEY

I can't say that I've paid that much attention to 'em before.

RIPLEY

The fish saved my life. Two years ago, I found out I had high blood pressure. So my doctor, he tells me to go get an aquarium, look at the fish every time I felt myself stressing out.

FOLEY

And the guy sent you a bill for this?

RIPLEY

It works. You should try it some time.

FOLEY

The next time I walk into a bank.

Ripley shakes his head, then gets up . . .

RIPLEY

Think about my offer, Jack.

Foley watches him go.

> BUDDY
> (*voice-over*)

Hey, Jack . . .

CUT TO:

Close-up of Foley as he turns to us.

> FOLEY

What?

We're inside a car across the street from the Kronk Recreation Centre – a red-brick building in a bleak, depressing neighbourhood.

> BUDDY

You see this one . . .

Buddy reads from a newspaper while Foley watches the gym.

'Fight over tuna casserole may have spurred slaying.' Seems this woman's live-in boyfriend, seventy years old, complained about her tuna noodle casserole and she shot him in the face with a twelve-gauge. Police found noodles in the woman's hair and think the guy dumped the casserole dish on her before she shot him. They'd been together ten years.

> FOLEY

Love is funny.

Buddy looks at him. Notices something over Foley's shoulder.

> BUDDY

Hey –

And now Foley turns and looks over as the black Town Car pulls into the Kronk parking lot.

INT. TOWN CAR. DAY

Kenneth and White Boy Bob nod along to some rap tape in the front seat. Glenn sits in the back, looking pale, hugging himself, shaking. Maurice looks out the window . . .

MAURICE

Was a time you see a gold Mercedes over in the parking lot has a licence plate on it say 'HITMAN?', you know Tommy Hearns is inside. Seeing the car would get our juices flowing.

Maurice looks at Glenn now and grins.

You already got your juices flowing, huh? Pissed your pants back there at Eddie's house, didn't you?

Glenn just looks at Maurice.

That was some shit, huh?

GLENN
(*indicates Kenneth*)
Why'd he have to do that to that girl?

MAURICE
Yeah, Kenneth, why you have to do that to that poor girl.

KENNETH
(*smiles*)

Do what?

Glenn says nothing, just looks at Kenneth.

MAURICE
Just wait till we get inside Ripley's house.

And he and White Boy Bob start laughing as they get out of the car.

GLENN
It's all right with you, I'll just hang in the car.

MAURICE
(*beat*)
No. You gonna stay close to me from now on. So you don't disappear on me.

GLENN

Why would I do that?

Maurice looks at him, starts laughing. White Boy Bob and Kenneth join in. Maurice leans over . . . Glenn flinches as Maurice opens Glenn's jacket so that we can see the blood splattered on his T-shirt.

MAURICE

Was worse than you imagined, wasn't it?
(*pause, smiles*)
Baby, you with the bad boys now.

INT. FOLEY AND BUDDY'S CAR. DAY

As they watch Glenn and Snoopy and White Boy Bob get out of the car.

BUDDY

Whatta you think?

FOLEY

I think Glenn opened his big mouth and now we got us another partner.

BUDDY

Or two.

INT. BOXING GYM. DAY

Glenn sits on a bench near the rear wall, facing the ring. Kenneth grabs a magazine, walks into the john. A shirtless White Boy Bob lifts weights while Maurice moves around the ring calling to the boxers inside.

MAURICE

Stick and jab!

VOICE

Hey, Studs, how you doing?

He looks up, sees Buddy and Foley coming this way.

GLENN

Jesus Christ, what're you guys doing here?

They sit down on either side of him, close.

FOLEY

Weren't you expecting us?

GLENN

That broad you picked up – did you know she was a US Marshal, for Christ sake?

Now he turns to Buddy as Buddy stands up, takes off his overcoat and sits down again.

She *knew* me from some bullshit dope bust. She drove me to court. Twice. You know what she said, we're in the car on the turnpike? 'I never forget anybody I've cuffed and shackled.'

FOLEY

Yeah? She said that to you?

Glenn turns to see Foley with a mild expression on his face, almost smiling.

What happened to your shades? Someone finally step on 'em?

GLENN
(*touches his head*)

I don't know . . .

Foley notices the blood on Glenn's shirt.

FOLEY

Who's blood you got all over you?

GLENN

These guys, man, they're crazy.
(*looks off*)

Shit.

Foley follows his gaze, sees Maurice coming this way, White Boy Bob beside him, carrying his shirts.

FOLEY

Is that Snoopy? In the purple doo rag?

BUDDY

What's he do now, tell fortunes?

Maurice stands at the edge of the ring apron, looks from Foley to Buddy and back again, pretty serious about it.

WHITE BOY BOB

We have a problem here?

MAURICE
(walking over)

Jack Foley, famous bank robber.

FOLEY

Snoopy Miller, famous fight thrower.

MAURICE

It seems to me I been reading about you in the newspaper. Busted out of some joint in Florida, huh?

FOLEY

Low class of people there, Snoop.

WHITE BOY BOB

You call him that again I'll put your head through the wall.

BUDDY

What? You mean Snoop?

MAURICE

Nobody calls me Snoop no more or Snoopy, is what White Boy's trying to say. He's a little crude, you understand. No, I left that Snoopy shit behind me.

BUDDY

But you call this bozo White Boy?

GLENN

White Boy Bob.
(baiting)
White Boy used to be a fighter.

BUDDY

What's he do now outside of shoot his mouth off?

White Boy Bob stares down Buddy, who couldn't give a shit.

FOLEY

Like being back in the yard, huh?

MAURICE

Just like it. Nobody backing down. You back down, you pussy. Tell me what you and Buddy doing up here in the cold?

FOLEY

Glenn didn't tell you?

GLENN

I thought you guys were busted.

FOLEY

Why? Just because you left us standing on the side of the road?

Foley looks at Glenn. Glenn shrugs, laughs nervously. Foley smiles, laughs with him, maybe a little too hard. Now Maurice starts laughing. Buddy, too. White Boy's lost, looking from one guy to the next as Foley gets up, faces Maurice, his smile going away as he says . . .

Look, Snoop, I don't know what Glenn promised you or what you think you're gonna get, but the deal is me and Buddy get half of whatever we take from Ripley, understand? How you and Glenn cut up the rest is up to you.

MAURICE

Let's go outside and talk.

FOLEY

What's the matter with right here? It's nice and warm.

MAURICE

Warm? Man, it's ninety-five degrees in here, sometimes a

hundred – the way Emanuel always kep' it so his boys'd sweat, get lean and mean like Tommy Hearns. No, I ain't talking any business in here. To me this is holy ground, man. You understand? I got to be someplace anyway. Y'all want to talk, come to the fights tomorrow night, we'll sit down and look at it good. The State Theater.

Foley nods, then looks at Glenn as Buddy gets up.

> FOLEY
> We'll see you tomorrow then.

Maurice then watches as they walk out.

> MAURICE
> White Boy, how much is the reward on the man again?

> WHITE BOY BOB
> Ten gees.

> MAURICE
> Uh-huh.
> *(pause)*
> You recall, did it say dead or alive?

EXT. CRIME SCENE. NIGHT

The same decrepit two-storey place Maurice et al. hit earlier. Now it's a crime scene. A small crowd of neighbourhood gawkers stand just behind the yellow tape. A huge spotlight lights up the front yard.

Karen pulls up in her rental car, gets out and badges the visibly freezing cop at the tape, working crowd control.

> KAREN
> I'm looking for Ray Cruz.

> COP
> He's inside.
> *(angry)*
> With everybody else.

Karen ducks under the tape and starts up the walk. She pauses to watch as two coroner's assistants cover with a sheet a dead black woman who lies just below a broken upstairs window.

INT. HOUSE. NIGHT

Hell. Karen has to step over a body minus a face that lies in the doorway. Straight ahead on the stairs is another body, a man on his back, head down the stairs, shotgun blast to the chest. He wears a dress, now bunched up around his waist.

Congealed blood runs down the stairs. Cops and crime-scene techs are everywhere. Karen looks at the guy on the stairs.

> VOICE
>
> Called themselves the Youngboys.

Karen looks over as Raymond Cruz, a stocky, genial-looking detective, comes out of the kitchen.

> CRUZ
>
> Ironic, isn't it?

> KAREN
>
> How are you, Raymond?

> CRUZ
>
> Freezing. But I'm getting warmer.

He kisses her on the cheek. She indicates the body by the door.

> KAREN
>
> Quite a mess.

> CRUZ
>
> Yeah. And I thought everyone liked Eddie.

> KAREN
>
> Who?

> CRUZ
>
> Dude in the dress is Eddie Solomon, used to buy scag off a corner till he kicked it and found his happiness with crack

and then started dealing himself. Word on the street was he was saving up for an operation.

                    KAREN
What is it with crack and transsexuals?

                    CRUZ
Yeah, Eddie was a real character. Had these girls cooked the rocks he called the Rockettes.

                    KAREN
Yeah. I saw one of 'em outside.

                    CRUZ
Yonelle. Looks like someone raped her, shot her, then threw her out the window.
                    (shakes his head)
Fuckin' animals.

This shuts them both up. Cruz indicates the door.

    Let's get some air.

She starts to follow him out, pauses as she sees something on the ground . . .

A broken pair of sunglasses. Wraparound . . . a lot like the ones she remembers Glenn wearing. Karen stares at them a moment, then walks out.

EXT. CRIME SCENE. NIGHT

As Cruz and Karen walk to his car. Strobes flash as press photographers struggle to shoot the crime scene.

                    CRUZ
Other than we had so much fun the last time we worked together. You gonna tell me why you're comin' to me instead of the FBI?

                    KAREN
I report to the FBI, first thing they're gonna do is ask me to go get some coffee.

CRUZ

You know, I'm not in homicide any more.

KAREN

No, I didn't know that.

CRUZ

Yeah, I'm crimes against persons and property now, also sex crimes and child abuse.

KAREN

Detroit, you must be pretty busy.

CRUZ

Yeah, and, as you can see, home invasions are big, too.

KAREN

Listen, Raymond, a year ago, DEA had this guy Glenn Michaels on possession with intent but couldn't make it stick. In his statement, Glenn said he went up to Detroit to visit a friend and look into job opportunities – if you can believe that.

CRUZ

Who was the friend?

KAREN

Guy named Maurice Miller, also known as Snoopy, a former prizefighter.

CRUZ

Christ, I know Snoopy Miller. He's a fuckin' wackjob thinks he's Sugar Ray Leonard. Hangs out with a couple other Grade-A nutcases over on the Westside.

KAREN

I'll need a last known address.

CRUZ

That's fine, but I don't want you to talk to Miller alone.

KAREN

Come on, Raymond, I'm a federal officer, I'm armed.

He turns and looks at her.

> CRUZ
>
> Yes, you are. I'll call you tomorrow with the address.

As he gets into his car, we then . . .

CUT TO:

*A newspaper. The crime scene from the night before. A shot of
Karen and Ray Cruz as they exit the house. A headline reads
'Triple Murder' blah-blah-blah . . .*

> BUDDY
> (*phone*)
>
> You have the paper?

INT. FOLEY'S HOTEL ROOM. DAY

*Foley, wearing a suit now, no shoes, no tie, looks at the
newspaper photograph of Karen.*

> FOLEY
>
> It's a terrific shot of her.

INT. BUDDY'S ROOM. DAY

Buddy looking at the same shot . . .

> BUDDY
>
> Outside of that.

Intercutting Foley and Buddy:

> FOLEY
>
> Doesn't say what she's doing up here, but I don't think it has
> anything to do with us.

> BUDDY
>
> She came up here on her vacation, 'cause she likes shitty
> weather.

*Foley reaches in one of the bags from the Jewish Recycling
Center and pulls out a tie.*

FOLEY

I think she's after Glenn. The girl still with you?

BUDDY

They don't stay the night, Jack, 'less you pay for it.

FOLEY

You tell your sister about it?

BUDDY

Just hung up.

FOLEY

How long you talk to her?

BUDDY

Two hours.

FOLEY

How long were you with the girl?

BUDDY

Forty-five minutes.

FOLEY

You didn't tell your sister about Ripley, did you? 'Cause I
don't wanna go through that again.

BUDDY

Forget about my sister. If Karen Sisco's tailing Glenn, we're
fucked. Tomorrow night at the fights we all get picked up.

FOLEY

Let's drive by where we're meeting and have a look. Maybe
take a look at Ripley's place while we're at it.

Foley hangs up. He faces the mirror, starts to tie his tie.

RIPLEY
(*voice-over*)
I guess next time I see you, you'll be wearing a suit and tie
. . .

INT. RIPLEY'S CELL. DAY

Foley leans in the doorway watching as Ripley, dressed in a jogging suit, and under the watchful eye of a guard, gathers up his belongings. He's going home.

> FOLEY
>
> I still haven't made up my mind yet.

> RIPLEY
>
> What's to think about?

> FOLEY
>
> You goin' right back to work?

> RIPLEY
>
> First, I'm goin' to Israel for a year, study the Talmud, work on a kibbutz . . . then come back, maybe take some tennis lessons.

He tears a picture off the wall . . .

> Here . . .
>
> *(hands it to Foley)*
> Something to remember me by.

Foley stares at the photograph of sea life.

> It's not the real thing, but it's still nice to look at.

Foley looks at Ripley, who extends his hand.

> See you on the outside, Jack.

INT. FOLEY'S HOTEL ROOM. DAY

Foley finishes tying his tie, stares into the mirror, takes in the overall effect.

> FOLEY
>
> *(smiles)*
> Hi! I just broke outta jail!

His smile fades, he then sits down heavily on the bed, looks at the picture of Karen another moment, then sets the paper aside, grabs the Yellow Pages, flips to hotels and dials the phone . . .

> VOICE
> (*phone*)

Atheneum Hotel.

> FOLEY

Karen Sisco, please.

> VOICE
> (*pause, then*)

I'm sorry, but there's no one by that name registered.

> FOLEY

Thank you.

He dials the next number . . .

> VOICE
> (*phone*)

Best Western . . .

EXT. MAURICE 'SNOOPY' MILLER'S HOUSE. DAY

Red brick, showing its age. Karen rings the doorbell and then waits with her hands shoved into the pockets of her dark navy coat. The door opens to reveal Moselle in her green silk robe holding her arms close against the cold.

> KAREN

Moselle Miller?

> MOSELLE

What do you want?

> KAREN

I'm looking for Maurice.

> MOSELLE

You find him, tell him the dog got run over and I'm out of grocery money.

> MALE VOICE

Moselle. Who you talking to?

MOSELLE

Lady looking for Maurice.

MALE VOICE

What's she want?

MOSELLE

Hasn't said.

KAREN

That's not Maurice?

MOSELLE

That's Kenneth, my brother. He's talking on the phone.

MALE VOICE

Ask what she want with him?

MOSELLE

You ask her. Maurice's business is none of *my* business.

Sounding tired or bored. She turns from the door and walks into the living room. Karen steps inside, pushes the door closed and steps into the foyer.

MALE VOICE

How do I know?

Karen peers into a study, a small room with empty bookcases, and sees Kenneth in his backward red baseball cap as he talks on the phone.

KENNETH

The State, huh. Who's fighting?

Karen walks into the living room, where Moselle sits on the sofa lighting a cigarette.

MOSELLE

You like to sit down?

KAREN

Thanks.

Karen takes a chair and looks around the room: dismal grey daylight in the windows, dark wood and white stucco, the fireplace full of trash, plastic cups, wrappers, a pizza box.

I'm looking for a friend of mine I think Maurice knows.

· MOSELLE
You not with probation, one of those?

KAREN
No.

MOSELLE
You a lawyer?

KAREN
(*smiles*)
No, I'm not. Maybe you know him. Glenn Michaels?

Moselle draws on her cigarette, blows out a stream of smoke.

MOSELLE
Glenn? No, I don't know any Glenn.

KAREN
He said he stayed here last November.

MOSELLE
Here? In this house?

KAREN
He said he stayed with Maurice.

MOSELLE
Well, *he* ain't even here that much. I like to know where he goes, but at the same time I don't *want* to know, you understand?

KAREN
(*beat*)
Your dog was killed?

MOSELLE
Got run over by a car.

KAREN

What did you call it?

Moselle looks at the couch, where a mangled frisbee sits.

MOSELLE

Was a she, name Tuffy.

KAREN
(*nods, then*)
Where do you think I might find Maurice?

MOSELLE

I don't know – the gym, the fights. I *know* he don't miss the fights. Having some tomorrow night at the State Theater. He use to take me.

KAREN

The State Theater?

VOICE

What you want with Maurice?

Karen turns, see Kenneth standing in the arched entrance from the foyer.

MOSELLE

She looking for a man name of Glenn.

KENNETH

Did I ask you? Go on out of here. Do something with yourself.

He waits until Moselle gets up, not saying a word, walks away from them through the dining room. Karen watches him come towards her now in kind of an easy strut. She indicates the scar over his eyes.

KAREN

You're a fighter?

KENNETH

How you know that?

KAREN

I can tell.

KENNETH

I *was* . . .

He moves his head in what might be a feint.

Till I got my retina detached two time.

He's standing so close to her, Karen has to look up at him.

KAREN

What'd you fight, middleweight?

KENNETH

Light to super-middleweight, as my body developed. You go about what, bantam?

KAREN

Flyweight.

KENNETH

You know your divisions. You like the fights? Like the rough stuff? Yeah, I bet you do.
(*moves closer*)
Like to get down and tussle a little bit? Like me and Tuffy, before she got run over, we use to get down on the floor and tussle. I say to her, 'You a good dog, Tuffy, here's a treat for you.' And I give Tuffy what every dog love best. You know what that is? A bone.
(*real close*)
I can give you a bone, too, girl.

KAREN

You're not my type.

KENNETH

Don't matter. I let the monster out, you gonna do what it wants.

KAREN

Just a minute.

Her hand goes into her bag next to the chair.

KENNETH

Bring your own rubbers with you?

Her hand comes out of the bag holding what looks like the grip on a golf club. Kenneth grins at her . . .

What else you have in there, mace? Have a whistle, different kinds of female-protection shit?

Karen pushes out of the chair to stand with him face-to-face.

KAREN

I have to go, Kenneth.

She gives him a friendly poke with the black vinyl baton that's like a golf-club grip.

Maybe we'll see each other again, OK?

She steps aside and brushes past him. He grabs her left wrist.

KENNETH

We gonna tussle first.

Karen flicks the baton and sixteen inches of chrome steel shoots out of the grip. She pulls an arm's length away from him and chops the rigid shaft at his head, Kenneth hunching, ducking away . . .

God *damn* . . .

He lets go of her and Karen gets the room she needs, so that when he comes at her, she whips the shaft across the side of his head and he howls, stops dead, presses a hand over his ear.

What's wrong with you?

KAREN

You wanted to tussle, we tussled.

And she walks out. She sees Moselle standing there in the foyer. Karen looks at her a moment, puts the baton in her purse and comes out with a business card.

I wrote my hotel number on there – in case you run into Glenn.

Moselle slips the card into the pocket of her robe. Karen smiles at her and walks out the door.

EXT. RICHARD RIPLEY'S HOUSE. DAY

It's snowing pretty hard when Foley and Buddy pull up out front.

INT. BUDDY'S CAR. DAY

Buddy wipes the condensation off his window, so they can see the house.

> BUDDY
> Now that's a really big house.

> FOLEY
> Jesus, look at that wall. Place almost looks like a prison.

> BUDDY
> No doubt the man's got some big-ass security system.

> FOLEY
> Time comes, we knock on the door. See if he wants to talk about old times. Go in the easy way.

> BUDDY
> Yeah? You think he'll let us in, we got Snoopy and the muscle-bound asshole with us?

> FOLEY
> Who says anybody's gonna be with us? I say we go to the fights tomorrow, find out what the Snoop's big plan is, then go in ahead of those guys – *alone.*

> BUDDY
> Let Glenn deal with the Snoop, while we're off livin' the good life.

FOLEY

Tell me something, Buddy. You know anyone who's actually done one last big score and gone on to live the good life? 'Cause it occurred to me that everyone *talks* about doing it, but I don't know anyone who's actually gone and *done* it. Do you?

BUDDY
(*beat*)
What about that D. B. Cooper guy?

Foley looks at him.

I mean, they don't know for sure he's dead.
(*pause*)
Look, there's always a chance we'll walk out've there with nothing. I say let fate decide.

FOLEY

Let fate decide? What're you, the fuckin' Dalai Lama now?

BUDDY

My sister believes in fate, but not hell. That's why she stopped praying for the lost souls since you don't hear that much about purgatory any more. But every day she asks her boss to pray I don't fuck up. Whatta you think, you think there's a hell, Jack?

FOLEY

Yeah, it's called Glades Correctional Institution and I'm sure as shit not going back there or any place like it.

BUDDY

You might not have a choice.

Foley looks at him.

They put a gun on you, you'll go back.

FOLEY

They put a gun on you, you still have a choice, don't you?

Foley turns back to the house. And now we hear . . .

MR HEARN
(*voice-over*)
I think you're gonna fit right in . . .

INT. RIPLEY ENTERPRISES PERSONNEL OFFICE. DAY

The personnel guy, Mr Hearn, sits behind his desk, squeezing a grip exerciser and smiling warmly at Foley, who wears a shitty suit and tie.

MR HEARN
Now Mr Ripley and I have had a long discussion about your role in the company and it was his feeling that you would be happiest working down here in Miami. How's that sound to you?

FOLEY
Great.

Mr Hearn pauses, looks down at Foley . . .

MR HEARN
You're about a 42 long, right?

FOLEY
What?

But Mr Hearn walks out without answering. Foley looks at the desktop, where a spoon sticks out of a half-eaten fruit-on-the-bottom yogurt, which in turn sits beside a half-eaten PowerBar.

Foley shakes his head, takes out his Zippo, starts to play with it.

MR HEARN
OK. Let's see how she fits.

Foley turns as Mr Hearn bounces back into the room with what looks like a uniform draped over one arm.

FOLEY
What is this?

MR HEARN
Your uniform.

FOLEY

My what?

Mr Hearn shows him the yellow patch that reads SECURITY *on one arm. Foley smiles . . . amused . . . angry . . . hurt . . .*

Are you kidding me?

INT. RICHARD RIPLEY'S OFFICE. DAY

View. Wet bar. Huge fucking aquarium.

RECEPTIONIST
(off-screen)

Sir, you can't go in there . . .

Ripley looks up from his desk as Foley steps in, the receptionist right behind him now.

RIPLEY

Jack? Whoa – what's the problem? Take it easy, let's talk . . .

Meanwhile, Ripley pushes a panic button beneath his desk.

FOLEY

A security guard? Are you fucking kidding me?

Ripley considers Foley a moment, then . . .

RIPLEY

You know, I wasn't sure you'd show up. But I was pretty sure that, if you did, you'd throw the job in my face.
(pause)
Understand something, Jack. Up to this point, everything you've done with your life means absolutely nothing in the real world. Less than nothing.

Foley says nothing.

You're a bank robber. This is not a marketable skill. There are no old bank robbers out in the world living on pensions. You know this. That's why you're here right now.

Still Foley says nothing.

Today, I'm offering you a lousy job at a lousy wage. You
think you're better than that? Fine. Show me. Show me that
you're really willing to change and we'll talk about
something better. A lot better. But first, Jack, you gotta earn
it.

FOLEY

How, Dick? The way *you* earned it? By marrying some rich
broad owns the company, selling it off a piece at a time, then
divorcing her? What is this Knute Rockne, pull yourself up
by the bootstraps bullshit? Back in prison, guy like you,
place like that, you were ice cream for freaks. You were a
goddamn dumpling. Maurice and a dozen other guys coulda
bled you till you had nothing. Till you *were* nothing. I saved
your ass. So you'll pardon me if I don't wanna sit on a
fuckin' stool all day saying 'Sign in here, please' or 'Hey, pal,
you can't park there.' OK, Dick? I can't do it.

RIPLEY

Jack, I'm disappointed. I guess I misjudged you.

Two massive security guards appear in the doorway.

FOLEY

Hey, what job he promise *you* guys?

GUARD

There's two ways we can do this.

FOLEY

Yeah? What are they?

RIPLEY

Gentlemen. I think we've calmed down now. Haven't we,
Jack?

FOLEY

Oh, yeah, I'm calm. In fact, I'm totally 'relaxed . . .'

And with that he picks up a paperweight (a lead fish) and wings it at the aquarium, shattering the glass.

EXT. RIPLEY'S BUILDING. FLORIDA. DAY

Foley is physically thrown out of the building by the two guards. He picks himself up. He kicks at the guards, who wave him off, go back inside.

Foley then starts down the steps, pauses as he sees . . .

The bank across the street we saw at the opening. Foley looks at it a moment, then calmly starts to take off his tie, drops it in the gutter as he starts across the street . . .

CUT TO:

INT. BUDDY'S CAR. DAY

As Buddy pulls away from the house, Foley pulls out the clipping of Karen he tore out of the morning paper. He's written the name 'Westin' on it.

> FOLEY
> Listen, I gotta get some better shoes, few other things before tomorrow. Why don't you drop me off at the Ren Cen, we'll hook up later?

> BUDDY
> Yeah, and I better call my sister.

CUT TO:

THE SNOWSTORM

It's really coming down. We then pull back to reveal we're looking out of a window inside the cocktail lounge at the top of the Westin.

A table of three young executive-looking guys in suits are laughing at something until Karen is ushered by a waitress to an adjacent table.

KAREN

Jack Daniel's, please, water on the side.

She turns, sees her reflection in the glass against the overcast sky, snow swirling, blowing in gusts, seven hundred feet above the city, down there somewhere.

EXECUTIVE GUY'S VOICE

Celeste, do us again, please, and put the lady's drink on our bill.

She turns to see them raising snifter glasses to her, smiling, pleasant-looking guys in dark suits.

KAREN

Thanks anyway.

WAITRESS
(drifting over)
They want to buy you a drink.

KAREN

I get that. Tell them I'd rather pay for my own.

She then watches the three guys looking at the waitress delivering the message. Then they look at Karen. She gives them a shrug, turns to watch the snow. Her drink arrives. She takes a sip, looks up as one of the guys comes over.

EXECUTIVE GUY

Excuse me. My associates and I made a bet on what you do for a living.

She glances at the table, the other two watching.

And I won. Hi, I'm Philip.

KAREN

If it's OK with you, Philip, I'd like to just have a quiet drink and leave. OK?

PHILIP

Don't you want to know what I guessed? How I know what you do for a living?

Tell you the truth, I'm not even mildly curious. Really, I don't want to be rude, Philip, I'd just like to be left alone.

She turns back to the snowstorm. She sees his reflection turn and leave. A moment later, the next one appears at the table.

SECOND EXECUTIVE GUY

I think I know why you're depressed – if I may offer an observation.

She just looks at him. So sure of himself.

I have a hunch you're the new sales rep and your customer isn't exactly knocked out by the idea of a young lady, even one as stunning as you, handling the account. Am I close? Hi, I'm Andy.

She says nothing to him.

ANDY

We're ad guys. We flew in from New York this morning to pitch Hiram Walker Distillery, present this test-market campaign for their new margarita mix. What we do, we show this guy who looks like a Mexican bandido, you know, with the big Chihuahua hat, the bullet belts –

KAREN

Andy? Really. Who gives a shit?

He gives her a sympathetic expression.

ANDY

Want to tell me what happened?

KAREN

Beat it, will you?

She stares at the guy until he turns away. She sips her drink, stares once more out at the blizzard. After a few moments, another dark suit appears, reflected in the window.

VOICE

Can I buy you a drink?

Boom. Not one of the executive guys. She stares at the reflection for a moment, then slowly turns, looks up at Jack Foley now standing there in his new navy-blue suit.

> KAREN
> *(beat)*
>
> Yeah, I'd love one.
> *(pause)*
> Would you like to sit down?

He pulls the chair out, looking at her. The three guys at the other table now staring as he sits down. Foley offers his hand.

> FOLEY
>
> I'm Gary.

She hesitates, then shakes his hand.

> KAREN
>
> I'm Celeste.

She smiles with him. When she lowers her hand to the table, his hand comes down to cover hers. She watches his expression as she brings her hand out slowly, his eyes not leaving hers, and lays her hand on his. The tips of her fingers brush his knuckles lightly, back and forth.

> It takes hours to get a drink around here. There's only one waitress.

> FOLEY
>
> I can go to the bar.

> KAREN
>
> Don't leave me.

> FOLEY
>
> Those guys bother you?

> KAREN
>
> No, they're all right. I meant, you just got here.

She picks up her drink and places it in front of him.

Help yourself.

She watches him take a sip, smack his lips.

> FOLEY
>
> You like bourbon?

> KAREN
>
> Love it.

> FOLEY
> (*passes the glass back*)
> Well, we got that out of the way.
> (*pause*)
> Tell me, Celeste. What do you do for a living?

> KAREN
>
> I'm a sales rep. I came here to call on a customer and they
> gave me a hard time because I'm a girl.

> FOLEY
>
> Is that how you think of yourself?

> KAREN
>
> What, as a sales rep?

> FOLEY
>
> A girl.

> KAREN
>
> I don't have a problem with it.

> FOLEY
>
> I like your hair. And that suit.

> KAREN
>
> I had one just like it – well, it was the same idea, but I had to
> get rid of it.

> FOLEY
>
> You did?

> KAREN
>
> It smelled.

FOLEY

Having it cleaned didn't help, huh?

KAREN

No.

(*pause*)

What do you do for a living, Gary?

FOLEY

(*beat*)

How far do we go with this?

This stops her, throws her off balance.

KAREN

Not yet. Don't say anything yet. OK?

FOLEY

I don't think it works if we're somebody else. You know
what I mean? Gary and Celeste, Jesus, what do they know
about anything?

KAREN

It's your game. I've never played this before.

FOLEY

It's not a game. Something you play.

KAREN

Well, does it make sense to you?

FOLEY

It doesn't have to, it's something that happens. It's like seeing
a person you never saw before – you could be passing on the
street – you look at each other and for a few seconds, there's
a kind of recognition. Like you both know something. But
then the next moment the person's gone, and it's too late to
do anything about it, but you remember it because it was
right there and you let it go, and you think, 'What if I had
stopped and said something?' It might happen only a few
times in your life.

> KAREN

Or once.

They look at each other a moment, then . . .

> FOLEY

Why don't we get out of here.

They both get up. The ad guys at the table watch as she follows Foley to the elevator. Karen winks at them.

INT. ELEVATOR. NIGHT

As they ride down to Karen's room. She looks at him, looks away. The doors open and they exit.

INT. KAREN'S HOTEL SUITE. NIGHT

He follows her in. She walks to the bar, fixes them each a drink. He checks out the room, takes in her view.

> KAREN

How'd you find me?

He comes over to her, takes out the newspaper clipping with her picture and shows it to her.

> Oh, God . . .

> FOLEY

I called your room from downstairs.

> KAREN

If I had answered, what were you gonna say?

> FOLEY

Well, I'd say who I was and do you remember me and ask if you'd like to meet for a drink.

> KAREN

If I remembered you. I came looking for you. I would've said sure, let's do it. But for all you knew I could show up with a SWAT team. Why would you trust me?

FOLEY

It would be worth the risk.

She looks at him, touches his face with her hand . . .

KAREN

You like taking risks.

FOLEY

So do you.

He kisses her now, puts his arms around her.

KAREN

What's the hurry, Jack? You have to be somewhere?

She hands him his drink. They both drink, then . . .

Sooner or later . . .

She stops and he looks at her over the rim of her glass.

You really wear that suit.

FOLEY

That's not what you were about to say.

She shrugs, lets it go. He puts down his drink, kisses her. She lets him, then moves to the couch.

KAREN

Remember how talkative you were? In the trunk? Adele said you do that when you're nervous.

FOLEY

She did, huh.

KAREN

You kept touching me, feeling my thigh.

FOLEY

Yeah, but in a nice way.

He sits down and they kiss again. This time she peels his jacket off. He does the same with hers. He's starting to unbutton her blouse when –

I might've smelled like a sewer, but you could tell I was a gentleman. They say John Dillinger was a pretty nice guy.

KAREN

He killed a police officer.

He stops. Looks at her.

FOLEY

I hear he didn't mean to. The cop fell as Dillinger was aiming at his leg and got him through the heart.

KAREN

You believe that?

FOLEY

Why not?

She looks at him, decides to get off this subject. Anyway he's finished unbuttoning her blouse and is now putting his hands inside her shirt. She closes her eyes.

KAREN

You know that Sig .38 you took was my favourite. My father gave it to me.

As he kisses her on the neck.

What were you gonna do with me?

FOLEY

I don't know. I hadn't worked that part out yet. All I knew was that I liked you, and I didn't want to leave you there, never see you again.

KAREN

You waved to me in the elevator.

She's loosening his tie, unbuttoning his shirt.

FOLEY

I wasn't sure you caught that.

KAREN

I couldn't believe it. I was thinking of you by then, a lot, wondering what it would be like if we did meet. Like if we could take a time-out . . .

FOLEY

Really? I was thinking the same thing. If we could call time and get together for a while.

They look at each other a moment.

You know I saw you on the street.

KAREN

Where?

FOLEY

Outside Adele's.

He starts to kiss her again, but –

KAREN

You were going to see her?

FOLEY

To warn her about Chino.

KAREN

So she did help you?

FOLEY

I don't think we should get into that.

KAREN

No, you're right. Or Buddy. I won't ask if he's with you or what you're doing here in Detroit. Or if you've run into Glenn Michaels yet.

FOLEY

Don't talk like that, OK? You scare me.

And he moves to kiss her, but she stands up, holds out her hand.

KAREN

Come on.

He gets up and she leads him across the room.

INT. BEDROOM. NIGHT

Jack sits on the bed to take off his shoes, stands up to take off his pants.

> KAREN
> Are you gonna leave your tie on?

He looks at her, down to her bra and panties, watches as she gets out of the rest of her clothes and comes over to him, standing close to help him with the tie.

> FOLEY
> My God, look at you.

When her clothes are off, she loops the tie around his neck again and then as she turns off the light . . .

She kisses him. He sits down on the bed, drawing her back with him, the only light now coming from the sitting room.

> You having fun?

She smiles and then they start to make love as we then . . .

FADE OUT

CUT TO:

Karen eyes open, serious now.

She's lying in Jack's arms. She looks at him a moment, then moves away from him to sit up and swing her legs off the bed.

> FOLEY
> You coming back?

> KAREN
> I'm just going to the bathroom.

She gets up and crosses the room to the bathroom and closes the door. Foley picks up his Zippo off the night table.

INT. BATHROOM. NIGHT

She comes in. Looks at herself in the mirror. Suddenly feels self-

conscious. She grabs a bathrobe off the door.

INT. BEDROOM. NIGHT

Foley lies there, fiddling with the Zippo, staring up at the ceiling. She comes out again and stands looking down at him.

> KAREN
>
> I want you to know something. I wasn't looking for just a fuck, if that's what you're thinking.

> FOLEY
>
> Why are you mad?

> KAREN
>
> Or I did it for some kind of kinky thrill. Score with a bank robber the way some women go for rough trade.

> FOLEY
>
> What about *my* motive? Now I can say I fucked a US Marshal. You think I will?

> KAREN
>
> I don't know.

He raises the covers, but she just stands there.

> FOLEY
>
> I know of a guy he goes in the bank holding a bottle he says is nitroglycerin. He scores some cash off a teller, he's on his way out when he drops the bottle. It shatters on the tile floor, he slips in the stuff, cracks his head and they've got him. The nitro was canola oil. I know more fucked-up bank robbers than ones that know what they're doing. I doubt one in ten can tell a dye pack when he sees one. Most bank robbers are fucking morons. To go to bed with a bank robber for kinky thrills, as you say, you'd have to be as dumb as they are. I know you're not dumb, so why would I think that? Why would *you* think I might think that?

She comes over and sits down on the bed.

KAREN

You're not dumb.

FOLEY

I don't know about that. You can't do three falls and think
you have much of a brain.

*They lie there for a few moments, Karen watching him. He senses
this, looks at her.*

You getting serious on me now?

KAREN

I'm trying not to. I just wanna know what's gonna happen.

FOLEY
(*beat*)

You know.

And he kisses her.

EXT. DETROIT. DAY

*The sun is out. The snow has stopped falling. A white blanket
covers everything.*

INT. KAREN'S HOTEL ROOM. DAY

*Karen opens her eyes, wakes up. She closes them again, lies on
her side, but doesn't move for a moment. Then . . .*

KAREN

Oh, for Christ sake, grow up.

*She opens her eyes and rolls on to her back. She turns her head:
Foley's gone. She gets out of bed.*

INT. SITTING ROOM. DAY

*Karen comes into the room tying her robe. She looks at the coffee
table where . . .*

Something wrapped in a napkin lies by the half-empty bottle and the ice bucket. She picks it up and slowly unfolds the 'gift' from Foley: her Sig-Sauer .38.

INT. FOLEY'S HOTEL ROOM. DAY

Buddy stands at the window looking out as Foley – in his underwear – sits at the table reading the newspaper, a room-service breakfast, a bottle of Jim Beam close by.

> BUDDY
>
> It took you, what, seven hours to buy a pair of shoes?

> FOLEY
>
> I saw Karen Sisco.

Buddy turns to him.

> BUDDY
>
> And she saw you?

> FOLEY
>
> Yes, she did.

> BUDDY
>
> So how's that work, a wanted felon socializing with a US Marshal?

> FOLEY
>
> You know how I felt about her.

> BUDDY
>
> Did you give her a jump? If you did I might begin to understand where your head's at.

> FOLEY
>
> It wasn't about getting laid. I just wanted to know what might've happened if things were different.

> BUDDY
>
> You find out?

> FOLEY
>
> Yeah, I did.

Buddy watches Foley pour a shot of Jim Beam in his coffee.

                    BUDDY
    So what's that mean? That you're disappointed by what you
    found or you're sorry you robbed all those banks?

                    FOLEY
    I don't know.

INT. KAREN'S HOTEL ROOM. DAY

*Karen sits there staring at a Wild Turkey bottle, a couple of
glasses. She reaches for the phone, dials. A moment later, we hear
Marshall Sisco's answering machine and she hangs up.*

INT. STATE THEATER. NIGHT

*A ring set up onstage. Men hang out on the side. Where movie
seats used to be are rows of round nightclub tables; a row of
them on each of four levels rising a step at a time up through the
theatre to the bar. Rap music booms out of speakers as fighters
are announced.*

*Everyone in here is black except for Glenn and White Boy Bob,
who sit at a table in the front row, while Maurice, in shades and
a dude black felt cap set on his head just right, walks along the
apron of the stage.*

                    MAURICE
    Stick and jab, stick and jab!

*White Boy Bob throws down a beer and gives Glenn's shoulder a
jab.*

                    WHITE BOY BOB
    You drink like a girl.

*White Boy Bob looks around to see if there are any other morons
sitting nearby who think it's funny. Kenneth comes through for
his pal and laughs.*

INT. STATE THEATER. NIGHT

Karen walks through the bar, pauses as she sees Glenn sitting with White Boy and Kenneth. She steps back into the shadows as Glenn glances anxiously about.

Glenn pushes his chair back.

> GLENN
> I got to go take a piss.

He hesitates, sees the car keys on the table in front of White Boy Bob. But before he can grab them . . .

> WHITE BOY BOB
> What're you telling us for? You want somebody to hold your little pecker?

Glenn gets up, sees his coat on the back of the chair, but knows he can't take it with him. He walks away from the table.

EXT. STATE THEATER – PARKING LOT. NIGHT

Glenn exits the theatre and crosses to the parking lot. Karen exits right after, watches him get into the Town Car.

INT. TOWN CAR. NIGHT

Glenn, behind the wheel, half-lying on his right side as he tries to rip open the locked glove compartment. His head jerks around as Karen opens the door. He sits up straight as she gets in with him.

> KAREN
> Glenn, are you trying to steal this car?

> GLENN
> Jesus, I don't believe it.

> KAREN
> Another one of those days, huh, nothing seems to go right?

He raises his empty hands.

GLENN

I don't have the keys.

KAREN

I see that.

GLENN

I mean I'm not stealing the fucking car.

KAREN

You're not?

GLENN

I already stole it. Last week or whenever it was, in West Palm. I can't be stealing it again, can I?

KAREN

The two guys you were with – that one, that isn't Maurice Miller, is it? I've seen Snoopy's mug shot and that didn't look like him.

GLENN

Jesus. How'd you know about Snoopy?

Karen looks at him, shakes her head.

KAREN

Glenn, I know your life history, who your friends are, where you've been and now, it looks like, where you're going. Put your hands on the wheel.

GLENN

You're gonna bust me for picking up a car?

KAREN

For the car, for aiding and abetting a prison escape, and conspiring to do whatever you came here for.

GLENN

Listen, these guys, they're gonna be out here any minute looking for me. They're fucking animals.

KAREN

What's going on, Glenn?

GLENN

Nothing. I just wanna get the fuck outta here.

KAREN

But I thought the whole thing was your idea?

GLENN

Rippin' off Ripley was my idea, but these guys, man, they're into shit I can't handle.

KAREN

Ripley? You mean the Wall Street guy?

GLENN

Yeah, the plan was to pick him up at his office tomorrow, take him out to his house in Bloomfield Hills. Now, I don't give a shit what they do.

KAREN

And is Foley a part of this?

GLENN

He's supposed to be, but he hasn't shown up yet, which is a good thing for him.

KAREN

Why's that?

GLENN

Maurice is gonna kill him, try and collect the reward.

KAREN
(*beat*)

But you say he hasn't shown up, you think he backed out?

GLENN

I don't know – he doesn't exactly confide in me.

KAREN

Gee, I wonder why not.

GLENN

I'm freezing my ass off.

KAREN

You want to get out of here, run, it'll warm you up.

GLENN

Really?

KAREN

But listen, Glenn. If you're lying to me . . .

GLENN

I know, you'll find me. Jesus, I believe it. I keep thinking if you hadn't driven me to federal court last summer, you wouldn't even know who I am.

KAREN

If I didn't know you, Glenn, by tomorrow you'd be in jail or dead. Look at it that way. Go on.

And he takes off. She sits there another moment, then flicks her cigarette out the door, gets out the car.

EXT. PARKING LOT. NIGHT

Karen looks across the street at the theatre, sees people leaving. A few seconds later, she steps behind a car and watches as Buddy and Foley pull into the lot.

INT. STATE THEATER. NIGHT

Maurice sits with White Boy and Kenneth as Foley and Buddy come down the aisle to their table.

MAURICE

Where you been? You miss the big boys, come in time for the walkout fights. Well, shit, you may as well pull up a chair.

Foley and Buddy remain standing.

Kenneth, this is Mr Jack Foley and this is Mr Buddy, famous bank robbers.

Foley nods to the raincoat draped over the back of a chair.

FOLEY

Who's sitting here?

MAURICE

Your homie, Glenn. Only thing, he went to the men's about a while ago and never came back.

Foley gives Buddy a look. White Boy Bob grins at them.

WHITE BOY BOB

I think he must've fell in.

MAURICE

I sent these two looking for him, they come back shaking their heads.

FOLEY

Well, if he left his coat and he's been gone a while.

WHITE BOY BOB

The car's still there. I looked.

MAURICE
(*to the ring*)

Reggie, push off and hit, man. Push him off.

FOLEY

We're leaving.

MAURICE

The fuck you talking about?

FOLEY

Snoop, if you don't know where Glenn is . . .

Maurice takes Foley by the arm, moves him away from the table.

MAURICE

Look, what you worried about Glenn for? What's he know?

FOLEY

I thought everything.

Foley watches the fighters: one of them patient, moving in while the other one takes wild swings and misses . . .

MAURICE

Glenn knows everything we suppose to do *tomorrow*. Glenn could tell somebody that, yeah, but it don't mean shit. You understand? 'Cause Glenn don't know I changed the plan.

(*pause*)

It's happening tonight.

Foley looks at Maurice now.

Soon as we leave here. Stop home and pick up what we need and go do it.

FOLEY

(*beat*)

Give me a minute, talk to Buddy.

MAURICE

You got two minutes, that's all. Make up your mind.

FOLEY

I wasn't asking permission.

Foley walks up to the bar with Buddy.

They want to go tonight, before Glenn gets in any trouble, opens his big mouth.

BUDDY

Whatta you wanna do?

Foley takes out his lighter, begins playing with it.

You know they gonna set us up.

FOLEY

I get that feeling, yeah.

BUDDY

But you still think you can get the diamonds 'fore they do?

Foley looks at him a moment, then . . .

FOLEY

I'll make you a deal. Get out of here. Right now. I'll do the job with the Snoop, meet you wherever you want and give you half.

BUDDY

Half for doing what?

FOLEY

Getting me out of Glades for starters.

BUDDY

And who watches your back?

CUT TO:

Maurice as he sits down with White Boy Bob and Kenneth, watching Buddy and Foley talk up at the bar.

MAURICE

Man has all that reward on his head and still talks like a con in the yard. You know what I'm saying? Like he's a man you don't mess with. Yeah, well, what I say to Jack Foley is buuull*shit*.

EXT. MAURICE'S HOUSE. NIGHT

It's snowing as Maurice, White Boy Bob, Kenneth, Buddy and Foley pile into the back of a van, the name of some plumbing and heating company on the side.

We pull back to reveal that we're watching from inside Karen's car. She waits for the van to pull away, then follows.

INT. VAN. NIGHT

Kenneth – the fucking maniac – at the wheel. Buddy and Foley piled into the back of the van full of plastic pipe and equipment. Maurice pulls on a pair of white coveralls.

FOLEY

That what they're wearing these days to break and enter?

MAURICE

Break and enter, shit. Take it and git, how it's done. Don't waste any time. That's how you do it.

> **FOLEY**
> So you've done this before, huh?

> **MAURICE**
> Shit, yeah. White Boy even got busted for it.
> (*pause*)
> White Boy, tell these boys the reason you went down on that burglary that time.

> **WHITE BOY BOB**
> I left my wallet in the house I robbed.

The guy grins at them. Foley can't believe it.

> **MAURICE**
> Takes the TV, the VCR, some other shit and leaves his wallet on the floor.

> **FOLEY**
> That's a wonderful story, Snoop. I'm very excited about tonight.

> **MAURICE**
> Hey. You learn from doing.

Foley and Buddy exchange looks. Maurice turns around, a Beretta in his hand. Foley looks at him. Buddy tenses.

> You know how to use one a these?

> **FOLEY**
> I've seen 'em used on TV.

Maurice hands Foley the Beretta. Then reaches into a bag, comes up with a .38 he hands to Buddy.

INT. KAREN'S CAR. NIGHT

Karen tries to keep up with the van. But with the snow and the way Kenneth drives, she starts to lose them. She speeds up around a corner and loses control of the car.

EXT. STREET. NIGHT

Karen's car does a 360 in the ice and snow.

INT. VAN. NIGHT

Buddy and Foley are jostled about the back from Kenneth's insane driving.

> BUDDY
> Slow down.

Kenneth grins in the mirror, punches it more. Buddy gets out the .38 and touches it to the back of Kenneth's head.

> Get ready to grab the wheel when I shoot this asshole.

Kenneth, his eyes freaked with speed, glares at Buddy in the mirror.

> MAURICE
> Do like he says, man. Slow down.

EXT. KAREN'S CAR. NIGHT

A pissed-off Karen gets out of her car, watches the van disappear.

> KAREN
> Shit –

INT. KAREN'S CAR. NIGHT

She takes out her cellphone, punches a number, reorients her car at the same time.

EXT. RICHARD RIPLEY'S HOUSE. NIGHT

The van creeps by one way, then the other, then pulls into the driveway.

INT./EXT. VAN/RIPLEY'S HOUSE. NIGHT

All five of them in the back end of the van now, bumping into each other until Maurice lets White Boy Bob out the rear end, leaving the doors open enough so he can watch. He then racks the slide on a .45.

MAURICE

'An army .45 will stop all jive.' Huey P. said that.

BUDDY

You think he was talking about walking into people's houses when he said it?

Maurice looks at Buddy. Buddy holds his gaze. Then the coach lights on either side of the front entrance come on.

MAURICE
(*pulls his mask down*)

Get ready to go skiing.

Now the front door opens . . .

Here we go.

We catch a glimpse of a woman in the doorway, arms folded over her bathrobe as White Boy Bob gives her a push and steps inside the house with her.

Maurice is out of the truck and Kenneth, with a shotgun, is scrambling to be next. Buddy catches him by his jacket collar and holds him squirming until Foley is out.

The minute Kenneth's feet hit the driveway he turns the twelve-gauge on Buddy, still in the truck. Foley takes the barrel in one hand and shoves it straight up in Kenneth's face.

FOLEY

Go on in the house before you get hurt.

Kenneth puts his face up close to Foley's and stares at him good before going inside. Foley turns to Buddy.

There's still time, take me up on my offer.

BUDDY

I'm not leaving you alone with these assholes.

INT. HOUSE. FOYER. NIGHT

Maurice has the woman back against a table. She's in her forties, with thick red hair hanging free. She looks ready to take a swing at whoever approaches.

                          WOMAN
      I work here. I'm the maid.

Kenneth reaches out, opens her robe and we get a flash of flimsy bra and low-cut panties before she slaps him away.

                       WOMAN/MAID
      Fuck off.

                         KENNETH
      Hey, shit, we're gonna have a party.

                         MAURICE
      Not yet. Where's Mr Ripley?

                           MAID
      I told you, he isn't here.

                         MAURICE
      Out for the evening?

                           MAID
      He's in Florida. Palm Beach.

                         MAURICE
                          (*beat*)
      When's he due back?

                          FOLEY
      Jesus Christ, what difference does it make? You want to wait
      for him?

                           MAID
      Mr Ripley's down for the season. Christmas to Easter.

                         MAURICE
      You here all by yourself?

                            144

MAID
(*beat*)

That's right, just me.

Foley catches the hesitation, glances at Buddy.

MAURICE

Where's Ripley's safe at, he keep his valuables in.

MAID

I don't have any idea.

MAURICE

Let's go upstairs, have a look at the man's bedroom. All right now, you and Mr Buddy check the rooms down here. Look at the wall behind any pictures hanging on it. Look at the walls in the closets. The man has a safe, it's gonna be up there somewhere.

FOLEY

How about his place in Florida? If you'd called, we could've checked his walls down there before we left. That is, if you'd checked to see where he was. You follow me?

Maurice gives him a look, then pulls the maid up the stairs. Kenneth and White Boy Bob follow.

MAURICE

You set off any kind of alarm and you're a dead Hazel. Understand?

Kenneth puts his arm around the maid.

KENNETH

What's you name, mama?

He hooks a finger in the waist of her panties, pulls on the elastic, is about to look in there when Maurice backhands him across the face.

MAURICE

First money, then pussy.

Alone with Buddy now, Foley rolls his mask up on his head.

FOLEY

You ever wear one of these?

BUDDY

I don't ski.

FOLEY

Stay with the maid. I'm gonna have a look around.

INT. KAREN'S CAR. NIGHT

Karen on the phone – snow falling all around her.

RAYMOND CRUZ
(*phone*)

I'll send a unit over there, see if there's anything going on.

KAREN

Tell me where Ripley's house is. I'll meet them there.

CRUZ
(*phone*)

Karen, you gonna promise me you're not gonna go in, do anything stupid till I get there.

INT. BEDROOM. NIGHT

Full of fat, cushy chairs and a sofa, everything white or black, a wet bar, a big TV, CD player. Buddy moves into the doorway, peers inside.

Kenneth is trying to find a radio station while Maurice and White Boy Bob ransack the place. White Boy Bob checks under the mattress.

WHITE BOY BOB

Hey –

Maurice and Kenneth look over expectantly.

I found a rubber.

MAURICE

White Boy, the man's not gonna hide no diamonds under the fuckin' mattress.

Maurice looks out the door, sees Buddy in the doorway.

Where's Foley?

BUDDY

Checkin' the other rooms, like you said.

MAURICE
(*to White Boy*)

Go keep an eye on him.

White Boy Bob slips out of the room. Maurice turns to Kenneth, who's still playing with the stereo.

Kenneth, fuck the radio, put on a CD.

KENNETH
(*looking them over*)

I don't recognize none of these bands.

MAURICE

Just pick one, put it on.

INT. HALLWAY (UPSTAIRS). NIGHT

White Boy Bob watches from the end of the hall as Foley peers into each of the bedrooms. Foley sees a back staircase and starts down. A moment later, White Boy Bob follows.

INT. HALLWAY (DOWNSTAIRS). NIGHT

White Boy Bob comes down the stairs. No sign of Foley. White Boy starts down one hallway, then turns back. Now he's lost. He opens a door, starts to walk into a closet, then backs out. He goes down the hall, turns into . . .

INT. KITCHEN. NIGHT

White Boy Bob enters, calls out tentatively.

Uh, Foley?

He takes in the huge room, the massive sub-zero refrigerator. He moves to the freezer, opens it, takes in the frozen steaks.

Cool.

INT. HALLWAY (DOWNSTAIRS). NIGHT

Foley quietly moves to the doorway, peers into the kitchen, watches as White Boy Bob starts going through the freezer, taking out steaks and stacking them up on the counter. Foley shakes his head and moves on.

INT. LIBRARY (DOWNSTAIRS). NIGHT

Dark. As Foley steps into the doorway, we boom down to reveal a lighted aquarium in foreground. He comes into the room, sits down in an armchair beside the fish tank.

He leans close to the glass, stares at the fish a moment. He sees a door reflected there and turns to look across the room, sees how the phone cord disappears underneath.

> FOLEY
> They cut the lines, Richard.

Silence. The door opens and we see a terrified Richard Ripley sitting on top of a toilet, the phone in his lap.

> RIPLEY
> Foley? That you?

> FOLEY
> How are you, Richard?

> RIPLEY
> Jesus Christ, what the hell are you doing here? What's going on? Who's upstairs?

> FOLEY
> Maurice Miller, couple of his friends.

RIPLEY

Maurice? From Lompoc? Good God.

Ripley moves to the doorway.

Have they got Midge up there?

FOLEY

What kinda man lets a woman answer the door, this time a night?

RIPLEY

We thought it might be her husband. Sometimes he comes and checks up on her. She told him I was down in Florida.

FOLEY

A minute or two, you're gonna wish you were.

Ripley looks at him. Foley pats the back of a chair.

Why don't you come on over here, sit down, Richard, have a look at your fish.

EXT. BLOOMFIELD HILLS. ROAD. NIGHT

Karen slowly negotiates her way through the snowstorm.

INT. BEDROOM. NIGHT

The music on loud (Herb Alpert – 'Tijuana Taxi'). Buddy stands in the doorway, watches Maurice, out of his coveralls, as he takes suits and sport coats from the walk-in closet to look them over. He tries on a coat, turns to the maid.

MAURICE

How do I look, mama?

MAID

Like a fag.

Maurice smiles at her, goes back into the closet. Kenneth stares at the maid, nodding slowly.

KENNETH

I think she like to tussle with me. Get boned a way she
gonna remember.

*She looks to the doorway, where Buddy now starts to take a step
into the room, when Maurice comes out of the closet . . .*

MAURICE
(*off-screen*)

Motherfucker!

He sticks his head out of the closet.

I found the safe.

Buddy backs out of the room.

EXT. RIPLEY'S HOUSE. NIGHT

*Karen drives slowly past the house. White Boy Bob emerges with
an armload of steaks and sets them on the front steps.*

MAURICE
(*off-screen*)

White Boy! Get your ass up here!

White Boy Bob hurries back into the house.

INT. LIBRARY. NIGHT

*Ripley sits on the couch across from Foley. He keeps looking up
at the ceiling.*

RIPLEY

What do you want from me, Jack? Name it. You want
money?

FOLEY

You gonna write me a cheque?

RIPLEY

We'll go to my bank. I'll make a withdrawal.

Foley just looks at him. Buddy sticks his head in the room.

BUDDY

They found the safe.

FOLEY

You remember Buddy, don't you, Richard?

BUDDY

Yeah, hi. Nice house.

RIPLEY

Thank you.

INT. BEDROOM. CLOSET DOORWAY. NIGHT

White Boy Bob comes in as Kenneth and Maurice are getting ready to blast the safe with the shotgun and pistol.

MAURICE

We gonna open up this fucker . . .

Maurice and his boys open fire on the safe. The maid covers up as bullets begin ricocheting all over the room.

Jesus . . .!

EXT. HOUSE. NIGHT

Karen sees the muzzle flashes in the upstairs window and quickly gets out of the car.

INT. LIBRARY. NIGHT

Buddy and Ripley look up.

RIPLEY
(*gets up*)

Good God . . . they're shooting Midge!

FOLEY
(*pushes him down*)

Siddown, Dick. They're trying to open the safe, not your maid.

INT. BEDROOM. NIGHT

Maurice, Kenneth and White Boy Bob get ready to fire again.

> MAURICE
> A'ight, this time we gotta get the motherfuckin' *trajectory* right . . .
>
> > (*pause*)
>
> OK, on three: one . . . two . . .

> MAID
> The combination is three–ten–forty-four.

They all turn to look at her, guns still pointing at the safe.

> Richard's birthday.

EXT. HOUSE. NIGHT

Karen cautiously makes her way towards the front door.

INT. BEDROOM. NIGHT

Maurice finally gets the safe open. They all anxiously peer inside. Maurice narrows his eyes, reaches in, pulls out one of three toupees. He stares at it.

> MAURICE
> . . . the fuck is this . . .

> WHITE BOY BOB
> Are they dead?

He looks at White Boy Bob.

> MAURICE
> Go find Foley. NOW!

INT. LIBRARY. NIGHT

Foley leans forward in the chair now.

> RIPLEY
> I can't believe you're still angry with me, Jack, after all this time.

FOLEY

I'm not angry, Richard.
(*staring at the tank*)
In fact, I'm completely relaxed. Thing is, I can't tell if it's the
fish that're cooling me out or all those uncut diamonds on
the bottom of the tank there.

Ripley sags, closes his eyes.

BUDDY

Damn –

*And now Buddy takes a closer look and now we, too, see that,
strewn about the bottom of the aquarium, are dozens of uncut
diamonds of various sizes.*

FOLEY

Dumbfuck Glenn was right, there's about five million worth
in there, wouldn't you say, Richard?

RIPLEY

Five point two.

BUDDY

They look like plain old rocks.

FOLEY

They sure do.

He gets up, looks at Buddy.

Go get a bag.

*Foley turns to Richard as Buddy comes back into the room with
a plastic bag, starts reaching into the tank.*

I were you, I'd get up and run.

RIPLEY

I'm not leaving Midge.

FOLEY

Don't be an asshole, Richard. They're gonna kill you.

RIPLEY

If that's my fate, so be it. I'm not leaving.
(pause)
I love her, Jack.

Foley looks at Buddy. Now what?

BUDDY

C'mon.

Foley just looks at Ripley, who doesn't move.

FOLEY

Good luck, Richard.

MAURICE
(off-screen)
Someone down here?

Buddy and Foley slip out the other door, down the hall, just as
Maurice walks in, some of Ripley's clothes over his arm.

Well, if it isn't the Ripper hisself.

RIPLEY

Are those *my* suits?

MAURICE

Where you been hiding, Dick?

EXT. HOUSE. NIGHT

A now-freezing Karen hugs a retaining wall, watches as Foley
and Buddy emerge from the house.

At the van Buddy leans under the dash. Foley looks up at the
house, where we see shadows moving about in the upstairs
window, hear the faint pumping of the music. We hear the van
start.

BUDDY

OK.

Buddy straightens up, looks at Foley.

Come *on*.

FOLEY

Shit.

BUDDY

What?

FOLEY

They're gonna rape the maid, aren't they?

BUDDY

From the looks of those boys, the Ripper too.

FOLEY

And then they'll kill 'em.

BUDDY

At least.

Foley looks at the diamonds in the bag.

FOLEY

We made it, didn't we?

BUDDY

All you gotta do is get in.

Again Foley looks at the diamonds, then . . .

FOLEY

I'm going back inside.

BUDDY

I'll go with you.

Foley finally hands him the bag with the diamonds in it.

FOLEY

No, you dump the van, meet me at the airport. I'll take one of Ripley's cars.

BUDDY

Jack –

FOLEY

Listen, Buddy, the shit that's about to go down, you'll be on the phone with your sister for a month. Let me do this part alone.

Buddy just looks at him.

I'm saying this isn't your problem. Far as I'm concerned, we're square.

Foley turns to go.

BUDDY

Hey . . .

Buddy hands him his gun. Foley takes it, stuffs it in the back of his pants, and then turns back to the house.

FOLEY

Now get outta here.

Focus on Karen as she watches Foley go back inside. A moment later, the van pulls out of the driveway. Karen makes a decision, starts for the side of the house.

INT. RIPLEY'S HOUSE. THE FOYER. NIGHT

Foley enters and we hear the maid scream. Foley starts up the stairs.

INT. LIBRARY. NIGHT

Maurice and White Boy Bob both have their guns to Ripley's head.

RIPLEY
(*hears the scream*)

Midge –

MAURICE

Forget about her. Tell me where the money's at.

RIPLEY

Foley's got it.

MAURICE

Where the fuck is Foley?

INT. HALLWAY (UPSTAIRS). NIGHT

Foley comes up the stairs, heads for Ripley's bedroom. The door is closed now.

FOLEY

Midge?

He steps to one side, is about to reach for the knob, when suddenly the door is blasted off its hinges.

INT. KITCHEN (DOWNSTAIRS). NIGHT

Karen comes through the door, hears the gunshot, stops cold.

INT. HALLWAY (UPSTAIRS). NIGHT

Foley steps into the doorway and we see Kenneth and the maid bare, both sitting up in bed, Kenneth racking the shotgun, the maid turning away from him, gathering the covers that hang off her side of the bed . . .

. . . and coming around to throw them like a net at Kenneth as the shotgun goes off and the covers catch fire as Foley pumps one-two-three shots into Kenneth somewhere under there.

INT. LIBRARY. NIGHT

Ripley tries to get away.

RIPLEY

Midge!

Maurice grabs him by the collar, spins him around and whips him across the face with his gun. He and White Boy Bob then both hit Ripley on the head until he goes down and stays down.

MAURICE
(to White Boy Bob)
You take the front stairs, I'll take the back.

INT. BEDROOM. NIGHT

The maid jumps up and drags the burning covers from the bed and sees Kenneth now, the bullet holes in his chest, and stares blankly back at him. She then looks at Foley.

> MAID
> (*cold*)
> Where's Dick?

> FOLEY
> Downstairs.
> (*pause*)
> But wait here. There's two more.

INT. HALLWAY (UPSTAIRS). NIGHT

Foley starts out of the room and immediately hears . . .

> WHITE BOY BOB
> Hold it, asshole!

Foley sees White Boy Bob at the bottom of the stairs.

> Drop the gun.

Nowhere to go, Foley has to comply.

> Now stay right there. Don't move.

White Boy Bob starts to jog up the stairs two at a time, all the while keeping his eyes fixed on Foley.

> Maurice! I got Foley!

INT. BACK STAIRCASE. NIGHT

Maurice starts up the back stairs.

> WHITE BOY BOB
> Maurice! Up here!

A moment later, Karen comes out of the kitchen into the downstairs hallway – just missing Maurice.

INT. STAIRCASE. NIGHT

White Boy Bob gets maybe half-way up when he catches a toe on one of the risers and pitches forward. Stupidly, he tries to break his fall with the elbow of his gun hand and ends up jamming his chin down on to the muzzle of his gun, which, unfortunately for him, goes off, firing a bullet through his head and killing him instantly.

To say the least, Foley is stunned by this freak accident. He stands there looking at the dead bulk on the stairs.

> FOLEY
> *(finally)*
> You learn from doing.

Foley bends down to pick up his gun and we see Maurice coming up the back staircase, his gun raised and now firing away.

Foley is forced to jump back behind a pillar as Maurice keeps firing at him, shots ricocheting off the pillar, the railing, the wall . . .

INT. HALLWAY (DOWNSTAIRS). NIGHT

Karen hugs the wall at the sound of the gunshots, sees Ripley lying on the floor of the study.

INT. HALLWAY (UPSTAIRS). NIGHT

We hear click as the breech opens on Maurice's now empty .45. Foley steps out from behind the pillar and calmly bends down, picks up his gun. Maurice still walking forward . . .

> MAURICE
> Jack, you don't use a gun, do you?

> FOLEY
> Not until recently.

> MAURICE
> *(still coming)*
> Nervous?

FOLEY

A little.

MAURICE
(getting close)

This kind of set-up, you don't have any idea what the fuck
you're doing – do you?

FOLEY

You're right. So why take a chance –

*Foley pulls the trigger. Click. Maurice hesitates, surprised that
Foley would pull the trigger, then the two of them at the same
time rush each other, begin a messy* mano a mano, *now using
their spent guns as bludgeons.*

INT. LIBRARY. NIGHT

*As Karen carefully comes into the room, Ripley lets out a low
groan. She's bending down to check him when her phone rings.*

INT. HALLWAY (UPSTAIRS). NIGHT

*Foley and Maurice grapple on the floor near the head of the
stairs.*

INT. LIBRARY. NIGHT

Karen answers her phone and checks Ripley.

KAREN

Hello?

CRUZ
(phone)

We're a few minutes away. Just sit tight, stay outta the house
till we get there, understand?

KAREN

O-K . . .

INT. HALLWAY (UPSTAIRS). NIGHT

Foley finally shoves Maurice down the stairs. Maurice rolls down a few steps, right over White Boy Bob, as Foley gets up, runs back to the bedroom.

INT. BEDROOM. NIGHT

Foley enters, goes straight to Kenneth's body, begins searching for the shotgun (lifting the covers, turning over the body, etc.) with no success.

>   FOLEY
> Shit . . .

INT. STAIRWELL. NIGHT

As Maurice attempts to prise the gun out from under the dead bulk of White Boy Bob.

INT. BEDROOM. NIGHT

Foley, exasperated, stands back up.

>   MIDGE
>   (off-screen)
> This what you want?

Foley looks to where Midge stands – now back in her bathrobe, but, more importantly, clutching the shotgun. Foley crosses and takes it from her, begins to stride out of the room, when –

> It's empty.

Foley just looks at her.

INT. STAIRWELL. NIGHT

Maurice finally rolls White Boy Bob over, grabs the gun.

INT. BEDROOM. NIGHT

Foley sticks his hand in Kenneth's coveralls, comes out with a shell, loads the gun, snaps it shut.

INT. STAIRWELL. NIGHT

Maurice cocks the pistol, takes a step up the stairs.

> **KAREN**
> (off-screen)
>
> Maurice –

Maurice spins around, points his gun down at Karen, now standing in the foyer, her own gun pointing up at him.

EXT. RIPLEY'S HOUSE. NIGHT

Raymond Cruz and several green-and-whites arrive.

INT. BEDROOM. NIGHT

Foley, about to exit, stops cold as he hears two gunshots, then a body fall.

He stands still. Not sure who was just shot. After a long moment, we then hear:

> **KAREN**
> (off-screen)
>
> Jack?

He sees Midge looking at him, closes his eyes, sags against the wall.

> I know you're up there.

INT. FOYER. NIGHT

Foley steps into the hallway, his ski mask now pulled down over his face. He holds Kenneth's shotgun in one hand and his pistol in another.

> **KAREN**
> Come on, Jack – don't.

> **FOLEY**
> Pretend I'm somebody else.

KAREN

You think I'd shoot you?

Foley brings up the pistol and the shotgun. And now we hear the sirens.

FOLEY

If you don't, one of those guys will.

KAREN

What're you now, a desperado? Put the guns down.

FOLEY

I told you, I'm not going back.

He raises the guns hip-high and we hear sounds behind Karen, but she's quick to raise her hand, though she doesn't turn or look around.

KAREN

Don't do this. Please.

They stand there staring at each other.

FOLEY

No more time-outs.

He raises the guns. She sadly shakes her head.

KAREN

You win, Jack.

She fires and he falls to the staircase, dropping the guns, grabbing hold of his left thigh. And now Cruz and several other cops enter. Karen motions them to stop.

CRUZ

Karen, I told you not to –

KAREN

Wait, I know him – OK?

She goes up the staircase to where Foley is lying and gently lifts the ski mask and looks at his sad eyes.

I'm sorry, Jack, but I can't shoot you.

> **FOLEY**
> You just did, for Christ sake.

> **KAREN**
> You know what I mean.

She glances about, makes sure no one can hear, then leans closer to him.

> I wish things were different. I'm sorry, Jack.

Foley looks like he's in pain. He watches as she walks back down the stairs. As a couple of uniform cops rush past her and pick up Foley, a shaky Ripley staggers into the foyer.

> **MIDGE**
> Richard!

She comes running down the stairs into his arms. They embrace. He looks at Foley over her shoulder.

> **RIPLEY**
> (*sympathetic*)
> Listen, Jack . . .
> (*but then*)
> What'd you do with my diamonds?

Foley just looks at him.

EXT. BUSY STREET. NIGHT

Buddy pulls the van into an alley. He jumps out, jogs back to the street and hails a cab.

INT. CAB. NIGHT

Suddenly gets in, bangs on the bulletproof glass.

> **BUDDY**
> The airport.

The cab pulls away. Buddy glances up front, then pulls the

Ziploc bag from his coat and holds it up. There's a bit of water in along with the diamonds. A tiny fish swims in the water. Something about this makes Buddy smile as we . . .

DISSOLVE TO:

EXT. KAREN'S HOTEL. MORNING

The sun is out. The sky is clear.

> KAREN
> (*voice-over*)
> They don't know yet if they want to bring him up on the homicides.

INT. KAREN'S HOTEL ROOM. MORNING

Karen on the phone. Her suitcase on the bed.

> KAREN
> I doubt if they will. The Bureau's put a detainer on him, so when they're through with him here he'll go back to Florida.

INT. MARSHALL SISCO'S SITTING ROOM. MORNING

Marshall on the phone.

> MARSHALL
> You gonna go get him?

> KAREN
> It's possible. Why?

> MARSHALL
> I was just thinking . . . you could have a nice time with him on the plane – like picking up where your interlude, or whatever you call it, left off. And then throw him in the can.

> KAREN
> He knew what he was doing. Nobody forced him to rob banks.

MARSHALL

My little girl, the tough babe.

Karen hangs up, stares thoughtfully out the window.

INT. PRISON CELL. DAY

Where Foley stands staring out of his window.

VOICE

Foley.

As Foley turns around and faces a federal marshal in the doorway, we see that Foley's hands and feet are shackled.

INT./EXT. PRISON STATION GARAGE. DAY

The marshal leads Foley from the building to where a black government van waits. The marshal helps Foley inside.

FEDERAL MARSHAL

Have a nice trip.
(looks off-screen)
I'll get the other one.

INT./EXT. VAN. DAY

Foley sits down, stares at the floor. He looks depressed. We hear the front door open, then close.

KAREN
(off-screen)

Jack?

He looks to where Karen looks at him through a steel grate that separates the front from the back.

I got you a present, something for the road.

She pushes a Zippo through the grate.

I have to take it away, though, soon as the ride's over.

Before Foley can say anything, the back door is opened once

*more and the marshal helps another prisoner – a black man with
a shaved head – into the back of the van.*

FEDERAL MARSHAL
Jack Foley meet Hejira Henry.

*An annoyed Foley stares at the guy as the marshal shuts the
door, then gets in up front with Karen.*

FOLEY
Hejira? What kinda name is that?

HEJIRA
Islamic.

FOLEY
What's it mean, 'No Hair'?

HEJIRA
The Hejira was the flight of Mohammed from Mecca in 622.

FOLEY
The flight?

HEJIRA
The brothers in Leavenworth gave me the name.

FOLEY
You were at Leavenworth, huh?

HEJIRA
For a time.

FOLEY
Meaning?

HEJIRA
Meaning time came, I left.

FOLEY
You busted out?

HEJIRA
I prefer to call it an exodus from an undesirable place.

FOLEY
(*interested now*)
And how long was it before they caught up with you?

HEJIRA
That time?

FOLEY
There were others.

HEJIRA
Yeah. That was the ninth.

FOLEY
(*really interested*)
The *ninth*?

HEJIRA
Ten, you count the prison hospital in Ohio I walked away
from.

FOLEY
You must be some kinda walker, Henry.

HEJIRA
Hejira.

FOLEY
And so now you're off to Glades.

HEJIRA
Apparently, yeah. I was supposed to leave last night with the
lady marshal, but for some reason she wanted to wait.

FOLEY
(*looks at Karen*)
She did, huh.

HEJIRA
Cheaper I guess, take us both down in one van.

FOLEY
Yeah, could be. Or maybe she thought we'd have a lot to
talk about.

Like what?

FOLEY

I don't know.

(pause)

It's a long way down to Florida.

Foley glances at her, then turns back to Hejira Henry and considers the guy; a smile on Foley's face, his spirits a little higher than when he first sat down, as we then . . .

CUT TO BLACK

Other screenplays and film books from *ScreenPress Books*.
All available with free post and packaging from *TBS Ltd*,
01206 255777

Contemporary British Cinema

ORPHANS
Peter Mullan   1 901680 30 4   £7.99

WAKING NED DEVINE
Kirk Jones   1 901680 29 0   £7.99

HIDEOUS KINKY
Billy MacKinnon   1 901680 25 8   £7.99

STILL CRAZY
Dick Clement & Ian la Frenais   1 901680 21 5   £5.99

MY NAME IS JOE
Paul Laverty   1 901680 16 9   £7.99

KEN LOACH FILMOGRAPHY
ed. James Oliver   1 901680 15 0   £6.99

SLIDING DOORS
Peter Howitt   1 901680 13 4   £7.99

LOVE AND DEATH ON LONG ISLAND
Richard Kwietniowski   1 901680 08 8   £7.99

NIL BY MOUTH
Gary Oldman   1 901680 03 7   £8.99

THE FULL MONTY
Simon Beaufoy   1 901680 02 9   £7.99

TWENTYFOURSEVEN
Paul Fraser & Shane Meadows   1 901680 07 X   £8.99

THE BIG SWAP
Niall Johnson   1 901680 18 5   £9.99

American Cinema

THE NINTH CONFIGURATION
William Peter Blatty & Mark Kermode
1 901680 20 7   £9.99

THE ORIGINS OF THE EXORCIST
William Peter Blatty   1 901680 34 7   £4.99

OUT OF SIGHT
Scott Frank   1 901680 23 1   £8.99

SLAM
Marc Levin   1 901680 27 4   £12.99

ONE FINE DAY
Ellen Simon & Terrel Seltzer   1 901680 01 0   £7.99